LIVING BEYOND LIMITS: THE TAO OF SELF-EMPOWERMENT

LIVING BEYOND LIMITS:

STILLPOINT
Publishing
A Division of Stillpoint International, Inc.
Walpole, NH

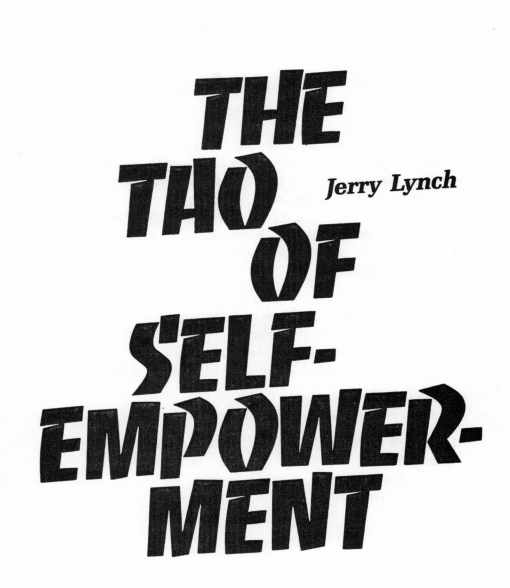

THE TAO OF SELF-EMPOWER-MENT

Jerry Lynch

STILLPOINT PUBLISHING
Books that explore the expanding frontiers of human consciousness
For a free catalog or ordering information, write:
Stillpoint Publishing, Box 640, Walpole, NH 03608 U.S.A.
or call 1-800-847-4014 TOLL-FREE (Continental US, except NH)
1-603-756-3508 or 756-4225 (Foreign and NH)

First Trade Edition

LIVING BEYOND LIMITS

This book is manufactured in the United States of America. Text design by Rostislav Eismont Design, Richmond N.H. Published by Stillpoint Publishing, a division of Stillpoint International, Inc., Box 640 Meetinghouse Road, Walpole N.H. 03608

Published simultaneously in Canada by Fitzhenry & Whiteside Ltd., Toronto

Library of Congress Card Catalog Number 88-060869
Lynch, Jerry
Living Beyond Limits
ISBN 0-913299-50-2

9 8 7 6 5 4 3 2 1

DEDICATION

To all the children in the world, especially to that little child within each of us who, when set free, is able to experience a wide, if not long, life.

PREFACE

It was a beautiful summer morning. My son Daniel and I were watching the little league team experience the joy and fulfillment of a baseball game. Proud parents were cheering for their children; children were cheering for themselves. And then it happened. A ground ball right at the first baseman—easy out to end the inning—rolled through his legs to right field. Two runs score. "Heckler, play first for Stevens," shouted the perturbed coach. Stevens sits embarrassed on the end of the dugout bench while the coach has a few words of harsh criticism.

My heart went out to that little boy that day. My three-year-old son asked a question I had difficulty answering in a way that could be understood: Dad, why is that boy crying? I had only stated that his feelings were hurt, knowing that I simply touched the tip of the iceberg. Of course, the repercussion of this incident would be felt well into adulthood by this child. Would he even try to play again after such humiliation? What messages did he internalize? Did he tell himself such things as I'm lousy, I can't play ball or I am worthless? How would this learned litany of self-imposed, limited affirmations, his poor self-image, his fear of failure, his vision of what he can or can't do, his choice of goals, his love and trust of others and self, his sense of personal power influence other aspects of his life?

Well, it has been said that joy and happiness, what we achieve and the direction we choose in life (relationships, jobs, fitness, schooling) have less to do with talent, abilities or opportunities than they do with how free we are of societal and self-imposed limits, taught to us from birth in both overt and subtle ways.

Also, personal emotional struggles in life (depression, stress, anxiety, pain, frustration, anger, financial concerns, relationship problems) are not necessarily the result of incurable inner wounds or deep-rooted psychological disturbance, but may occur from the lack of an ongoing, workable personal path that transcends these struggles. Life's difficulties, for most of us, I notice, arise out of an attempt to conquer, control, fight, change and resist the way things are—the way of nature—the way life is meant to be. For example, nature's way suggests that it is impossible to be loved and approved of by all people. Therefore, to not accept this natural law is to cause ourselves much pain. (Gandhi, Christ and Mother Theresa had enemies, so why shouldn't we?)

LIVING BEYOND LIMITS will enable you to examine and transcend self-imposed obstacles through the restoration of harmony, balance and alignment with the laws, ways and wisdom of nature. In the process, joy, happiness, self-reliance and fulfillment will become those cherished by-products that most of us have tried unsuccessfully to attain via external, material paths. LIVING BEYOND LIMITS, a book for all people of all ages, offers an educational, internal, body-mind-spirit journey that will facilitate transformation from a place of SCARCITY to a place of ABUNDANCE. It will re-ignite the personal power you experienced at birth by creating an awareness of the way of nature—how things happen—and by offering transformational tools for acting accordingly on the job, in the home and in all aspects of your personal life.

To help you accomplish this, I have made every attempt to create a meaningful blend and synthesis of various disciplines, including Eastern philosophies and religion, the martial arts, universal wisdom, and cutting-edge theories and practicalities from the field of psychology.

In Part One, *CREATION*, you will be introduced to the concept of the Chinese TAO and the laws and ways of nature; the inner journey is proposed as a way to re-create harmony with nature's way. You will learn how we were created with unlimited potential and how we, in fact, create our own limits.

Part Two, *RESTORATION*, discusses the specific ways we limit ourselves in all aspects of life and offers practical tools and strategies to help you move beyond such obstacles. This awareness into action approach will teach you to become aware of how nature works, how things are and how to act accordingly to increase your chances for fulfillment in every aspect of your life.

What would it be like if unlimited living were experienced? Part Three, *TRANSFORMATION*, presents a model of such living so that you can determine when you are on the path of nature. The concepts are a summarization of all the principles outlined in this book, and they are presented in a cohesive, readily available format to enable you to see that it's a basic, simple plan. However, staying on the path is quite a challenge and requires a constant vigil. But then again, fulfillment can only be obtained when we notice our patterns and adjust them accordingly.

A final thought: As a student of the Japanese martial art aikido, I am well aware of the harmony and balance that naturally occur between the YIN and YANG (the feminine and the masculine). Aikido has a wonderful way of blending the female and male within all of us. It allows you to go beyond those limitations, as defined by stereotypical roles, and challenges you to discover the balance. There is room in the art to express both sides of your human nature. And because the art of aikido is performed on a mat, a simple exercise pad, it is there—perhaps more than any other place—that I am offered the opportunity to be the person, the total human being, I am.

Unfortunately, the English language is not yet flexible enough to offer a single, collective word that encompasses the true spirit of the total person. Attempts have been made but not without contrived, awkward results. Therefore, I trust you understand my message that we are limited only by our imaginations—our minds—not by whether we are male or female. Throughout my book, I use the word person whenever possible; you will know I mean both male and female when I am obliged by the restrictions of the English language to use he or him to represent all of us.

ACKNOWLEDGMENTS

*T*o a truly gifted man and friend, John Visvader, whose teachings of Chinese Taoistic principles encouraged me to "notice," for the first time, the way of nature, the Tao. Life will never be the same

To a very special, wonderfully sensitive Taoist "master-in-residence," my son Daniel, who continues to force me to "notice" and teaches me to live according to the Tao. It's been a joy I never knew existed.

To an extremely insightful, loving and supportive spouse, Jan; you insisted for years, in spite of much resistance on my part, that we bring a child into this world because you unselfishly believed it would be good for me. Two children later and I wonder: How could I have resisted such an incredible gift? You helped me live the Tao and my life has entered a new dimension because of that.

To Georgia Fitzgerald for her loyal assistance in preparing the manuscript.

CONTENTS

INTRODUCTION

It all started in a philosophy class back in college (way back!). I was required to read a story that, unbeknownst to me at the time, would powerfully affect the rest of my life. The story, by the French scholar and existentialist Jean-Paul Sartre, was entitled *No Exit*. As I remember it, some people were trapped in a metaphysical, self-imposed "hell"—one room, no windows, crowded together and not able to leave. After much time in "hell," a door opened and they were free to go; however, they chose to stay because they feared the unknown. They had become comfortable with their horrendous lives.

I wasn't "comfortable" with mine. I was about to leave behind four of the most unpleasant years of my youth. Why didn't I leave sooner? Why hadn't I taken this philosophy course during the first quarter? I was miserable, unhappy and terribly unfulfilled. Yet, like those people in Sartre's story, I feared the unknown. I learned valuable, although costly, lessons from my experience: Never put up with anything that doesn't give you joy, happiness and fulfillment. Take the risk to discover what might be gained. Risk change;

dare to be fulfilled! Do not limit yourself. I have followed these philosophies from the moment I became aware of them at the age of twenty-one.

Although filled with joy, my life hasn't been without its upheaval and chaos. But I've grown to view such turmoil as the dues I pay for a life filled with a vast variety of experiences. A life of well-being and excitement is only possible if you are willing to take the risk and create fulfilling opportunities. The challenge in your world is not to search for total bliss and guaranteed happiness. They don't exist. The challenge is to accept nature as it is, to be courageous enough to live in this world with all of its paradoxes and limits, to go for what you deserve, and to open your heart and absorb the process. The challenge is not to change the world as much as it is to transform your attitude, beliefs and views about how it is, the way it is. You can discover its beauty, richness and power without trying to conquer and control all its errors and failures. Even they are filled with value, if we can just NOTICE.

Change is not easy. When we're given the tools, we must use them diligently. If you purchase a hammer, saw, nails and wood, and leave them in the garage, the fence will not get built. If you want a glass of milk, I don't advise pulling up a stool in an open field and waiting for a cow to back into your hands. Russian novelist Dostoyevsky once said, "A new philosophy, a way of life, is not given for nothing. It has to be paid dearly for and is only acquired with much patience and great effort." When he said "paid for," I'm sure he didn't mean the price of the book! As in the examples mentioned above, it would be foolish to buy this book and leave it on the shelf. It is a tool to be used for the construction of a life that goes beyond limits; and that journey requires vigilance and patience. The payoff is a life of well-being, excitement, love and fulfillment, a life that comes from working *with* nature, as you were meant to, rather than against it.

1 5

PART

CREA-

At birth, we are all in harmony with joy with unlimited potential. Then, with all of its beliefs, fears and atti- the grand plan. The chapters in this and how things are. They shed light experience fulfillment in life, only to with the universal way and instead, turmoil, anxiety and pain.

ONE

TION

nature, created in a state of complete
after years of exposure to the world
tudes, we become misaligned with
section reflect upon nature's way
upon how we were designed to
lose our original, natural connection
unwittingly, create a life of inner

FROM WHERE WE CAME

CHAPTER ONE

THE WAY OF NATURE: AN INNER JOURNEY

*Living in accordance with natural hierarchy
is not a matter of following a series of
rigid rules or structuring your days with
lifeless commandments——The world has order
and power and richness that can teach you how
to conduct your life artfully, with kindness
to others and care for yourself.*

Chogyam Trungpa
(Tibetan Buddhist scholar and author)

The ancient Chinese book of wisdom, the *Tao Te Ching*, teaches that every one of us possesses an incredible power or potential that is constantly available when we become aware of and align ourselves with the force of nature, the way things happen that is beyond our control. If we notice how these forces work, and act accordingly, life can be quite fulfilling. However, the price we pay for trying to control, fight or resist these natural patterns is a life of struggle and trouble. For example, rubbing your hand vigorously against the grain on a slab of redwood could ruin your afternoon. Slicing turkey breast against the grain creates an aesthetic disaster. Fighting the ocean current can be exhausting and futile. As a matter of fact, nature demands that you always go with the flow in anything you encounter; if we fail to act accordingly, problems ensue.

Although written twenty-five hundred years ago, supposedly by the scholar Lao Tzu, the *Tao Te Ching* continues to influence all of the world with its remarkable insights into the nature of life. For example, the Taoists believed that aligning yourself with the way of nature increased the possibility for personal growth and fulfillment. Such harmony results in the creation of enormous personal power and a sense of abundance. I can honestly say, after many years in the profession of psychology, that struggle, fear, frustration, disappointment, unhappiness and depression are rarely related to deep-rooted, psychological disadvantages. Such difficulties seem to arise out of our attempts to control, resist, fight, change and conquer the natural flow of life, the way it was meant to be. Failure to harmonize with "the way" can change your world from abundance to scarcity, from unlimited to limited. There is so much to lose, so it seems, from interfering with the natural states of people and events. R. L. Wing's translation of the *Tao Te Ching*, the *Tao of Power*, states it so well:

> Those who would take hold of the world and act on it,
>   Never, I notice, succeed.
> The world is a mysterious instrument,
>   Not made to be handled.
> Those who act on it, spoil it.
>   Those who seize it, lose it.

Aligning ourselves with the way of nature is perhaps best exemplified in the Japanese martial art aikido in which an opponent is defeated by the force of his own attack. The advantage of going with the flow, or non-resistance, can be demonstrated by the aikido exercise of the unbendable arm:

> Extend your right arm; hold it rigidly in front of you; make a fist.
>
> Ask a strong opponent to bend it. (This should be no problem for him.)
>
> Extend your arm once again; hold it out relaxed yet firm, pointed at a specific spot in the distance; visualize the forceful power of water pushing out of your arm like a fire hose, with the water hitting that spot; your hand is open and your fingers are in alignment with your straight arm.
>
> Ask the opponent to bend it. (It should now be more difficult to do.)

The lesson: *Resistance does not create positive results.* We need to flow with the way things are meant to be. Observe what happens to a pine tree during a huge snowstorm. The branches fill with snow and are susceptible to cracking because they remain rigid, whereas a willow tree branch will bend when weighted by snow, and release the heavy load, bouncing back to its original position unharmed.

Observe a young child and an adult skiing down a hill. Notice how each handles a fall—the child rolls with the direction of force; the adult stiffens, desperately trying to conquer, fight and resist the inevitable. The child laughs, gets up and continues down the slope; the adult waits for a stretcher.

To bring harmony and fulfillment to your life, you must consider these lessons and begin to comprehend the way of nature. Observing nature's laws teaches you to develop personal power in an unlimited fashion, provided you act accordingly. There are no mistakes on this path, just lessons. You will no longer try to put a round peg in a square hole. Without effort, the square hole welcomes the square peg. This is the Chinese concept of *wu wei*, non-force, let it happen. In his humorous account of the principles of Taoism in the *Tao of Pooh*, Benjamin Hoff talks about the "Pooh Way" (a pun on *wu wei*): "Those who do things by the Pooh Way find...things happen in the right way...when you let them; when you work with circumstances rather than saying, 'this isn't supposed to be happening this way,' and trying to make it happen some other way." Eventually, if you are blending with nature, with the way things work, all things will work out in a way that is appropriate for your life, regardless of what you may think about the outcome. (Even though it may not seem right at the time—outcomes can be strange.) Often-times, in the future, you will get the "A-HAH experience": "A-HAH! That's what was happening. That had to happen this way because of this." It couldn't have come out better even if you had tried or forced and pushed for what you thought was the "right" way. Things work out! This is the Tao. Accepting the truth of the laws of nature, trusting our perceptions of the world, relying on our instincts and intui-tion, balancing our extremes and harmonizing with the flow will all contribute to feelings of personal freedom, security, self-reliance, self-acceptance and personal power. These are the essential ingredients that can enable you to go beyond what you think are "limits" to experience true abundance and fulfillment in your life.

What is this "way of nature"? What are its laws? Anyone familiar with the Tao knows that it cannot be adequately described in words. Its meaning is unlimited: To define it is to limit it. It applies to everything; you just have to NOTICE. The Tao is an attitude of awareness about life's events as they occur. Simply NOTICE the way you may or may not work with whatever happens each day. If you are happy, you are probably in harmony with life and nature's way.

The following examples demonstrate a few of the ways of nature, how we become misaligned and the result of such disharmony. The examples are simply models from which to get reference points in order to facilitate the awareness process of how nature works.

THE WAY OF NATURE: Errors, setbacks and failures are an inevitable outcome of an expansive, fulfilling life. They cannot be avoided.

MISALIGNMENT-IMBALANCE: The perfectionist takes the attitude that errors and mistakes are abominable and can be avoided. The effort required to avoid errors in turn creates even more errors. Failure is also perceived as a limit that can be conquered.

OUTCOME OF IMBALANCE: Tremendous frustration, anger, disappointment and possible depression result from trying to avoid failure.

HARMONY WITH NATURE: Errors, setbacks and failures will still occur, but they will be viewed as unlimited opportunities from which to learn and forge ahead and, in the process, be fulfilled.

THE WAY OF NATURE: Changes and cycles in life are constant. The only real security that one can count on is that change will occur, that nothing remains the same.

MISALIGNMENT-IMBALANCE: One relies solely on work, relationships and home to offer security, always fighting the up-and-down cycles of life in order to resist change at all costs.

OUTCOME OF IMBALANCE: A loss of what one perceives as "security" is created. Struggle, frustration, unhappiness and anger are the result.

HARMONY WITH NATURE: Understand that life is a "rollercoaster" and, like nature, has its own seasons of change. The rhythms of life give us times to plant, harvest and rest. Things come and go; we only need to flow with them.

THE WAY OF NATURE: Aging is a natural process of life, with each stage of growth having a significant purpose.

MISALIGNMENT—IMBALANCE: Aging can be delayed, if not prevented, by face-lifts, hair dyes, wigs, clothing and other external remedies. Tremendous effort is made to fight and control the process.

OUTCOME OF IMBALANCE: Lower self-esteem, poor self-image, frustration, insecurity and unhappiness result over one's inability to control aging.

HARMONY WITH NATURE: Aging is a challenging process with unlimited opportunity for exciting personal growth, power, fulfillment and the attainment of wisdom.

THE WAY OF NATURE: Having fun, being spontaneously playful, is a vital part of daily living; it re-energizes the body, mind and spirit.

MISALIGNMENT-IMBALANCE: Play is only for children; it does not fit into the life of the serious adult. Fierce attempts to avoid or discount the process of free time are made.

OUTCOME OF IMBALANCE: Lack of joy, job burnout, irritability, anxiety, stress and relationship difficulties result.

HARMONY WITH NATURE: One understands that play is a necessary component of the growth cycle. Attention to the mind-body's need to vary activities will create the balance required for fulfillment and gratification.

THE WAY OF NATURE: Intimate friends and close relationships are important aspects to personal growth and fulfillment. Harmony with life is impossible without them.

MISALIGNMENT-IMBALANCE: There is no need for involvement with relationships. One attempts to resist, avoid and fight the natural tendency to establish close contact with others. One lives and works alone, refusing to take risks with intimacy.

OUTCOME OF IMBALANCE: Relationships, when they exist, become unhealthy, which, in turn, causes depression, illness, degenerative disease, and a basic sense of scarcity and lack of joy. Loss of self-love and bitterness toward life in general, result.

HARMONY WITH NATURE: One understands that life has more options, alternatives and directions when others are included. Love and intimacy become a major antidote to stress and anxiety. Giving to others is more fulfilling than trying to "go at life" alone.

In his beautiful translation of the *Tao Te Ching*, R. L. Wing makes the point that if you do not follow the way of nature with its uncompromising laws, if you do not follow the Tao and try to control or go against the grain, the Tao will remain indifferent. The path, for such individuals, will be a difficult one. "Excessive ambitions and desires," Wing points out, "divide people from their inner natures and from one another. Following the Tao requires no special knowledge...it is merely listening to the inner voice...holding to the path of least resistance."

THE INNER JOURNEY
The fundamental, basic tenet subscribed to in this book is that fulfillment in life is an inner journey of going beyond what you *think* are limits (as opposed to real limits, tested and proven to be so) to create abundance in all ways, rather than scarcity. This is best accomplished by combining the path of least resistance with the laws of nature in order to harmonize and blend with the way things are.

Recently, I asked a forty-two-year-old client of mine what he thought fulfillment might be. His reply: "I need a BMW, a condo on the beach and a gorgeous mate...then I'll have it all." I knew at that moment, I was in for a long afternoon. There is nothing wrong with his idea of fulfillment. So many of us desire a nice car and home, wonderful relationships and security, and these are fulfilling and possible. But something is missing.

First, what do you do in the meantime before these externals arrive? I think of the words of Alan Watts, talented scholar of Eastern thought and philosophy: "You don't dance to get to the other side of the floor." Second, there's no guarantee that the possession of these externals will answer your request for the "good life." How often I receive the prize only to be disappointed. I remember thinking how wonderfully fulfilling life would be if only I had my doctorate in psychology. After four years of sacrifice, avoiding Jerry, his wife and child, while at the same time giving my all to people who couldn't care less and used my talents for their own advancement, I graduated with the common "double-D" prize: diploma and divorce. And, in addition to this, who was I and where was I going? The answers to those philosophical questions took another ten years of "internal schooling." That journey continues and fulfillment has now become defined in a different way: The bottom line is the quality of the journey's process. Fulfillment is a daily experience. "Am I happy now?" is a question to be asked every day.

This new way has brought me much joy in everything I do. I might not have met my idea of a perfect friend, yet the important thing is to not limit myself NOW. I must focus on what love and closeness I can experience with those whom I know at this moment. Harmony and balance with my present world is the key to fulfillment; focusing on the future to include certain external amenities will simply create problems and unhappiness.

Although the inner journey is a personal adventure, I do not wish to imply that it is a "solo journey," without support, guidance or help. It is simply a call to create inner peace, harmony, balance, joy, love and fulfillment at home, on the job and with relationships; this may require support from others to help stay on the path. Books, tapes, seminars, support groups and organizations are available to keep our efforts honest and on target.

To further clarify this point, think of an EXTERNAL journey as being a temporary solution to fulfillment. That great relationship including sex twice a day will create tremendous joy. Yet such temporary well-being will create only temporary happiness. The internal journey, although at times appearing temporary, will always keep the progress of your life flowing with harmony. You might experience a step backward, but there will always be an accompanying two steps forward. This is the remarkable "DANCE OF LIFE" so easily observed in infants when they seem to take one step backward before taking two important steps forward. To accept this ever-present dance with its rhythmic steps is, in itself, the balance between being stabilized and moving forward. Expect the dance, and blend with its rhythm—IT'S LIFE! To try to control this movement is to experience struggle. Wisdom is to be happy knowing that control is not possible in much of our life.

Again, this means a complete change in attitude for many of us. To give away control is frightening. However, I believe it is much more frightening to hold on to the belief that we have control when we really don't. It's truly an illusion to think we can control outcomes at any time if we try hard enough. You can, however, control the choices you make and your views of the outcome, and this is the work of the INNER journey. Your heart does not transform with a new car, relationship or home. It changes only when it begins to see things according to the way of nature, the inner self.

The inner journey of fulfillment is like taking an exciting river-raft trip. It has a beginning and an end. It changes direction and, at times, seems to be going back to the start. The pace quickens rapidly through the narrows yet dramatically slows as the river widens. Sometimes the water is clear, sometimes murky and cloudy; exhilarating yet placid; raging yet calm. If you try to slow down when it speeds up, you struggle; if you speed up when it slows down, it will resist. You can't push the river. Paddle upstream and frustration will take over. You can choose to end the trip at any time, but you will do so at your own risk. The most exuberant journey is to give yourself over to the power of the river, and you will experience wonderful inner joy and fulfillment as it is meant to be. If you could see the river's path (your inner journey) from a higher perspective, you would see clearly that there is a beginning and an end, a natural progression and flow. And like the river, life is a journey with ups and downs, turns and surprises, cloudy and clear times. Let it flow! You need to trust—it's a must if limits are to be transcended and fulfillment obtained.

CHAPTER TWO

FROM UNLIMITED BEGINNINGS TO BEGINNINGS OF LIMITS

*We are conditioned to believe that
there are certain rigid limits to what we can
do and achieve. We are bombarded constantly
from both with limiting suggestions. Belief
in limits creates limited people. Once we
get over preconceived ideas about limitations
we can be so much more.*

Dr. Georgi Lozanov
(Researcher in Human Potential)

ature provided you and me with the potential to experience incredible joy, happiness and fulfillment; and it appears that we have gone out of our way to destroy that gift. Can you recall a wonderful period in your life in which you experienced total harmony and balance with nature, having all of your needs met? Remember the secluded home next to the water; food, drinks and accommodations were supplied free of charge; water and air temperatures were ideally comfortable. Every day was filled with pleasure, playing and "sleeping in" as late as your spirit willed. There wasn't any conflict, struggle or frustration; no stress, anxiety or tension. One big harmonious existence with all around you. You were there for almost a full year—in utero, enjoying the bliss of fulfillment. Then you were born.

And you are born, virtually unlimited, into a state of complete harmony with nature. Of course, life isn't total bliss, and you soon discover that the air temperature drops twenty-five degrees while some stranger pats your butt, and crying becomes a disturbing yet necessary communication device to get your needs met. Yet amid the radical and often unpleasant changes, you manage to "flow," to "go with the grain," and blend with your new home. You are basically fulfilled; abundance is yours for the time being. You don't "act on the world" or "seize it," so you don't lose it either. You simply blend—live in it, with it. When you are unhappy you express this clearly, and if your parents want harmony with their "new" world, they'll try to meet your needs. Taoist philosopher Chuang Tzu made the observation thousands of years ago that "the baby looks at all things all day without winking...he merges himself with his surroundings and moves with it. These are the principles of mental hygiene." To me, this is the bliss and fulfillment expressed by those who do in fact live in harmony with nature.

As you grow, people remark how wonderful your life is (assuming your environment hasn't begun to push its craziness on you—but it probably has). "Oh, to be a child again" is often heard. George Bernard Shaw once commented that "youth is wasted on the young." That is, you don't ever realize how great, how fulfilling, life is when you are a child. Some of us do, however, in spite of outside pressure to "mature," and take along these wonderful childlike qualities that help us maintain personal harmony with nature.

I'm beginning to believe that wisdom is the realization that the highest stage of maturity and development is the ability to maintain our childlike qualities. The ancient Taoists always encouraged the elderly to return once again to the state of childhood—a state of joy, harmony, freedom and fulfillment. What I notice about my friends is that those who appear happy, those who have a healthy outlook on life, are those who laugh, play and act childlike; they even look like kids. Of course, blending with the boardroom or courtroom or classroom environments may require modulating their enthusiasm for fun. Yet this, too, is a kind of harmony. It can be the game of adulthood, as long as you don't take yourself too seriously.

The child, therefore, serves as our model of what it's like to be unlimited, fulfilled. I asked my three-year-old son Daniel, "What do you do in pre-school?" To which he responded: "I'm a fireman who flies like Superman." Such joy! Imagine responding to the ubiquitously boring cocktail party question, "What do you do?" with "I'm an astronaut." The child can be anything; the child has no illusions about what he or she cannot do until the "evidence" has been collected. The adult criticizes and judges the possibilities before the limits have been tested. In the words of George Bernard Shaw, the child will "dream things that never were and ask 'why not?'"

The child possesses those wonderful qualities that most of us unfulfilled adults would love to recapture, qualities that create a blend with the way things are, the way nature is. Observe a child for two hours and notice how much you learn from him about the principles of alignment. The adult mimicking the child would experience all of the following:

> *playing* without a purpose or goal
> expanding options by becoming totally *curious*
> observing the world *without judgment* of self or
>   others
> being creative without the *fear of mistakes or failure*

3 0

cultivating a *sense of humor* and not taking oneself so seriously

daydreaming and creating fun fantasies for a more positive existence

giving love *unconditionally*, without fear of being used

focusing more on the *here and now* to eliminate guilt and worry

allowing for *intuitive* responses and behaviors, and doing what feels good more often

visualizing your ideal life and doing things to create it

silencing those illusions of such beliefs as: "I can't" or "I'm too old"

relaxing when necessary to recoup your vital energies (take a nap, perhaps)

observing more often than not—NOTICING!

This is the world from which the child doesn't care to escape as we do from our "adult" (a dolt?) reality. We have lost touch with the way and have become limited by what it means to be a mature human. For most of us, we seem to be sleeping away our time and need to relight the fire of fulfillment.

In the words of the English poet William Wordsworth, "The child is the father of the man." One interpretation of this is that our children give us the opportunity to observe and remember what we once had and how to recapture it. This is so beautifully demonstrated when we once again observe the difference between a child and an adult falling. Following the Taoist concept of "non-forcing" (*wu wei*), the child does not resist falling but goes with the flow, yields to nature, cries from shock yet rises unharmed. Refusing to blend or harmonize with nature's "calling," the adult fights, forces and tries to control the inevitable, thereby causing chaos, confusion, imbalance and a broken limb. Outcomes depend upon how willing we are to blend with these natural occurrences. Our human potential has been limited by our modern ways and methods; our lives are unsatisfying as we struggle with these ways. We need to consider the possibility of restoring fulfillment by harmonizing and blending with the way things are, not as we think they should be.

One of the most fulfilling and incredible experiences that has ever happened to me occurred recently. It never happened before and I doubt it will ever happen again. I walked five miles from home to obtain a quart of homemade applesauce. I love it so much. When I arrived at the store, they were sold out. Disappointed, I returned home and reminded myself that nature has its way. It wasn't meant to be. After ten miles of walking, I arrived near my house only to be greeted by a neighbor I hadn't seen for weeks. She called me into her house because she wanted to give me a jar of applesauce she had just freshly made. I now have an affirmation that says, "GO WITH THE FLOW LIKE H_2O." Observe and notice where

---

UNLIMITED LIVING

HARMONY, BALANCE WITH "THE WAY"
▼
ABUNDANCE
▼
FULFILLMENT ⟶ EXPERIENCE:
▼
love
excellence
happiness
courage
vision
self-direction
health
optimism
effortlessness
positiveness

nature takes you. Failure to do so will result in serious limitations to what is possible, and your chances for fulfillment will rapidly diminish.

There you have it—UNLIMITED BEGINNINGS! Unlimited in the sense that we are basically free to examine what we think are our "limits," as taught to us by society, and free to do something about those "limits." For example, you can make a switch in attitude from "I can't" to "I can." The former belief posture is one of those self-imposed limits that creates obstacles to fulfillment; it represents the BEGINNING OF LIMITS. Before examining how limits are created, the following diagram will attempt to clarify, side by side, the differences between unlimited and limited living. Our goal is to create a journey where we live beyond limits and experience what we all deserve: fulfillment.

LIMITED LIVING

RESIST, CONTROL, FIGHT "THE WAY"
▽
SCARCITY
▽
UNFULFILLMENT ⟶ EXPERIENCE:
▽
fear
perfection addiction
unhappiness
timidity
personal myopia
self-deception
illness
depression
struggle
negativity

BEGINNINGS OF LIMITS

WHAT IS A GIRL?—Born with a little bit of angel-shine...motherhood dragging a doll by the foot...stubborn, spry, sly, soft, mysterious mind. A little girl likes new shoes, party dresses, small animals, dolls, dancing, kitchens, tea parties, coloring books.

WHAT IS A BOY?—A delightful creature...found everywhere; climbing, swinging, running, jumping. A boy is truth with dirt on his face,...bubble gum in his hair and a frog in his pocket. He likes comic books, knives, trains and fire engines...fun out of trees, a sling shot and supersonic code ring.

When do you suppose such limited views and beliefs toward children were popular? Perhaps the 1950s? Things have changed, haven't they? Don't we now have a more expansive, less narrowing concept of children and what they can and can't do? Apparently not. I excerpted these two descriptive narrations, typed on pink and blue paper, respectively, from the birth package presented to neophyte parents at a "modern" southern California hospital in 1987. When does society begin to teach us attitudes, beliefs, fears and concepts that limit? Immediately! We need to consider options and alternatives for our children and expand our limiting views as to what they can do. It should be perfectly fine if my son Daniel desires to dance, play with dolls, attend a tea party— or for any little girl to collect frogs and climb trees.

Society is quick to create boxes for people to fit into, neatly labeling each one according to some predetermined, limited role. The danger in such action is that we tend to behave according to these limited labels. It is called a SELF-FULFILLING prophecy, and it has been established that such narrowing expectations predict future behavior. *What you believe about yourself will tend to be acted upon.*

Although you are born unlimited, society, as you can see, doesn't waste any time infusing its limited beliefs and attitudes into your abundant living. It is an insidious process that teaches you, over a period of many years, to function far below your capabilities. Most of us use a mere ten to fifteen percent of our full potential, whether it be at work, at play or in relationships. Our basic "modus operandi" is from a position of scarcity (a client of mine reminds me that it's "scare-city"). "I can't," "it never can be," "I never could" and "I don't have enough" become the litany of our limited language. This army of societal and self-imposed dictators constantly determines the path you choose—what you can or can't do. To live a life of scarcity is to live a life contrary to the grand design of nature—abundance.

My first memorable experience with limitations began at the age of seven. I received my first report card from school. In the parochial school where I was a student, getting a report card marked the most important day, scholastically speaking, in one's life. I knew I had done well and was excited to see the results. Five A's and one B. Bravo! I was proud to show my dad who, after scrutinizing the grades, pointed to the "B" and asked, "What happened here?" I was devastated. I had failed to live up to his expectations. Would he still love me? "I wasn't good enough" became my constant internal affirmation. I remember being unhappy for quite a while after the experience—seven or eight years, at least. I saw myself as a kid who didn't measure up. I began to believe in limited ways, to be afraid to take risks. I became a perfectionist, bent on "making up" for those lost years, only to become tense, stressed, disappointed and frustrated because perfection is an addictive illusion that cannot be attained. The failure cycle was spinning. I carried this posture into my early forties before things finally became clear.

What "significant others" tell us when we are children has a powerful effect on our chances for fulfillment. Oftentimes, the message is subtle and pervasive. As I tell you about my dad, I realize I often teach Daniel sets of irrational limits that initially appear to me to be perfectly rational limits. For example, like all children, he has no illusions as to what he can or can't do (according to the great Houdini, limits of any kind are an illusion), until all the objective data is collected to convince him one way or another (unlike you or I who decide upon what's possible based on "evidence," rather than feelings).

With this in mind, I relate the time he hit a ball high into a tall bush. It was dusk and rapidly getting darker. I said to him, "Let's go home; we'll never find it." His reply: "Yes we will; here's my bat. Get the ball." Knowing the improbability of finding it, I appealed to his rational mind: "It's too high up; I can't reach it"; logically responding, he proposed that I get a ladder. "No, Danny, it's too dark (I'm running out of reasons—limits); we'll not be able to see it." To which he quickly replied, "I'll get the flashlight you bought me." At this point, I "wake up" and tell myself, "Jerry, what are you teaching him? What is the message?" I take the flashlight, put it into the hedge, and eight inches from my head is the ball. "See, Daddy, I knew you could do it." He was right. Even if we didn't find it, we tried, and only by doing that can any of us determine the extent of our limits. The important lesson for me is to be vigilant with regard to those times I say, "No way, I can't." Fulfillment comes not from being able to do all things; it's the attitude that anything "can be" until proven otherwise. Such an unlimited stance opens up a world of possibilities. That's the way things are. It's the way of nature. To do otherwise is to create a misalignment and seriously hamper your chances for going beyond societal and self-imposed limitations. Living without limits is seeing all the potential possibilities in your life, professionally, socially, personally, athletically, spiritually, and saying "why not?"

How many of you remember the great professional football player, Jim Brown? In his day, no one came close to touching his abilities. He was the epitome of the unlimited athlete. One day, he visited a hospital to motivate and encourage kids who were severely sick. He came upon one little boy who was suffering from a debilitating disease, rickets. The boy looked up to "Big Jim" and told him that some day, he would break all of Brown's football records. That boy was O. J. Simpson and, as you know, he rewrote the record books for professional football running backs.

Do you have any limits? If so, where do they reside? To the best of my imagination, I can't imagine any limits. When I question those that appear to be obstacles, I begin to learn that I simply "think" they are so. Naturally, I am not referring to actual, rational, realistic limits: People can't fly (we've tried and haven't succeeded), dogs can't talk and I can't lift a twenty-story building. Short of these types of limits, anything should be considered possible. If you claim that "it can't be done," maybe you just don't want to do it. If you can't ski because you're too awkward, tell that to the expert skier with no legs; if you're "just not musical," tell that to the concert guitarist with no arms; or if you're "not coordinated," tell that to the little boy with rickets.

There is nothing more you need other than what you possess to become happy, joyful and fulfilled in this life. You simply must consider a change in attitude and let go of self-imposed limits. When I work with people who appear to be successful and happy, they don't have any special gifts, talents or qualities to which you don't have access. The key ingredient is their ability to go beyond the hampering obstructions.

Richard Bach, author of the bestseller *Illusions*, said that if you "argue for your limitations...sure enough, they're yours." Assume no limits until you try.

You are now ready to examine and transcend limits. In Part Two—RESTORATION: *What You Can Do*, you will discover specific laws of nature, how you misalign with them and suggestions for recapturing the unlimited self on your path of fulfillment. Certainly, there are many limits that we create and I don't pretend to address all of them. I have, however, chosen those areas that seem to affect all of us most of the time. I believe that many of the ways we limit ourselves can be subsumed under these categories. Since true personal power and potential for fulfillment are the result of noticing how nature works, and thus acting accordingly, the chapters in Part Two will attempt to follow this theme. Using a "triple A" approach, each chapter will begin with a discussion of a particular universal law, truth or wisdom (AWARENESS-THE WAY-THE TAO). We'll then look at how we create disharmony or misalignment with such principles (ABANDONMENT OF THE WAY). And finally, the chapter will explore various practical possibilities for acting in the ways of restoring the harmony, balance and alignment with natural events as they occur in your professional personal and spiritual lives (ACTION-ALIGNMENT WITH THE WAY). In the words of the Chinese poet and philosopher, J. Cheng, "It's simple but it ain't easy." You will need to do some honest work in the process.

PART

RESTO

As the title suggests, this part will with the laws of nature for the pur- fulfillment in this life. Each chapter closely related sections: first, a dis- nature and how we become aligned and strategies that will help to restore accordingly. As you will observe, by the work of Lao Tzu and his the *Tao Te Ching*, as well as other and martial art.

WHAT

TWO

RATION

help in the restoration of harmony
pose of experiencing joy and
is divided into two distinct yet
cussion about a particular law of
with "the way," followed by tools
alignment and enable us to act
this section is greatly influenced
ancient book of Chinese wisdom,
appropriate Eastern philosophies

WE CAN DO

CHAPTER THREE

BEYOND LIMITED VISION: THE ULTIMATE SKILL

He who cherishes a beautiful vision, or lofty ideal in his heart, will one day realize it. Your vision is the promise of what you shall one day be.

James Allen
(*As a Man Thinketh*)

VISION AND THE WAY OF NATURE

ne of the more truly amazing stories to come to us from the P.O.W. camps of Viet Nam is about a Navy pilot, incarcerated for many years. To occupy his time constructively and maintain a form of sanity, he decided to concentrate upon learning to play a musical instrument. He had never touched a guitar in his life, and he wasn't about to be presented with one at that time. So he and a buddy drew six lines on a two-inch-wide flat stick (mimicking the neck of a guitar) and presto—a musical instrument that would be the envy of every champion flat-pick guitarist in the world. For the duration of his stay at the "Hanoi Hilton," he compulsively practiced under the tutelage of his cell mate, a professional musician himself. He would "hear" the sound of certain music and voice the corresponding notes. His teacher would then show him the appropriate finger position on the "neck" corresponding to those notes. He memorized the chords and visualized, while in bed, the sequence of actions to "produce" the desired results. Following years of visualized practice, he was released from prison and returned home as an accomplished guitarist with his sanity intact.

Volumes of books could be filled with such powerful stories of visualization; such imagery is nothing more than nature's way of influencing actions and behavior. This universal principle of nature teaches that what you "see" in the "mind's eye" strongly influences what you get or achieve. Most outcomes are determined by the visions that preceded them. Although this is not true in all situations, the frequency with which outcomes are influenced by your images warrants serious consideration. Although you cannot control circumstances as they happen, you can shape the outcome of such events by the thoughts and visions you choose to have. For example, envision yourself during a job interview: Images of failure will create stress, tension and anxiety and, as a result, performance will suffer; imagine "flying" through the interview and you'll be calm, clear and confident—the necessary ingredients for a successful experience.

Remember the dream that woke you in a state of extreme fright, your palms sweaty and heartbeat elevated? It seemed so real, yet it's only another example of the how the body and mind work together in harmony to create reality.

Close your eyes for a minute. Imagine a juicy, sour lemon. Cut a wedge from the fruit and bite down, letting the sour juices permeate your mouth. Salivate? For sure—another case of the outcome being affected by the image.

In actuality, the way of nature is such that the central nervous system does not discriminate between real or imagined events. Therefore, whatever you choose to image will greatly determine the direction in which your life will flow, how you feel and the way you behave, act or respond. The implications of this natural act for fulfillment are enormous because most of your joy is affected by positive images. Naturally, this doesn't assume that fulfillment is simply a matter of thinking in such terms; there are other variables that are required. However, if the mind is out of balance with positive possibilities, the chances for gratification are increasingly more difficult. In this sense, our limits in life become defined partly by the images we choose to dwell upon. Let's see how this happens:

IMAGES OF MISERY (NEGATIVE). . .

lower interest and motivation to create a new existence

prevent the exploration of positive possibilities

create anxiety, tension and fear, thus hindering performance

IMAGES OF FULFILLMENT (POSITIVE). . .

raise hope and motivation to create a workable existence

reduce fear and create positive mental statements and images of success

improve performance and allow you to feel in control and to take initiative

Clear examples of limits that result from misalignment with this law of vision are the images conjured up when you either worry or experience guilt. In the former case, you become obsessed with images of disaster, catastrophe and other negative thoughts about circumstances that may never even occur, yet this leads to much immediate discomfort. With guilt, you become equally concerned with events that can't be changed, and this results in stress, anxiety and much unhappiness. In both cases, the images created are responsible for the feelings you experience, even though you clearly have no control over the outcome of future events or past occurrences. No amount of guilt or worry will change a thing, but it can cause much unnecessary pain and unhappiness.

So, images of fulfillment activate psychological processes that put you on the path to create a positive reality. To become misaligned with the way of nature, choose images of misery that contribute to the possibility of diminished joy and fulfillment.

Let me anticipate a question I am often asked: "Isn't it dangerous to get my hopes up at the risk of being disappointed? Maybe I should prepare for the worst and if it turns out OK, great." My answer is a resounding NO! It's true that focusing on a negative expectation will prevent disappointment; however, such thinking also contributes to a negative outcome that wasn't necessarily inevitable. Disappointment will not kill you; why not increase the likelihood of positive results?

This law of nature is often questioned because of the lack of "scientific proof" for its existence. You just need to notice how things work and decide for yourself. The next time you awaken from a night's sleep and feel physically and emotionally down, observe how the rest of the day evolves. Notice how you behave according to these negative images ninety percent of the time (see chapter on Personal Power). Do you want to wait until all the data is in that proves what you already know about the power of images, and continue to pay the price for misalignment?

This issue of "scientific proof" is always a "hot" one for Carl and Stephanie Simonton, who have had remarkable results with childhood cancer control. They use visualization for physiological self-regulation, in addition to other traditional therapeutic modalities. Dr. Carl Simonton tells a story about a psychiatrist who wrote to some of the leading scientists in the world asking their help in determining what constitutes scientific proof. One of the replies simply stated, "The question is too difficult for me," and he proceeded to state that he doubted he could make a significant contribution to such a complex issue. The letter was signed "Albert Einstein."

So, with this tale in mind, I proceed to align myself with the way nature is in regard to vision and the power it has over our chances for joy and fulfillment. I like to contemplate again the words of the wonderful George Bernard Shaw: "Some people see things as they are and ask 'why?'; I dream things that never were and ask 'why not?'" The key word is to dream—to visualize—a life of harmony and balance, one that is fulfilling. Once again, this is a call to return to one of those "childlike" behaviors alluded to earlier in the book. Children dream every day about wonderful things happening (assuming the environment is supportive). They dream they can do or be anything; acting out these fantasies is an expression of joy. Again, notice a child at play. Even mere observation will create momentary happiness for you, the viewer.

VISUALIZATION AS A PROCESS

There is a difference between "visual thinking" and the process of visualization. The former is a random, unconscious attempt to think about some future event or situation. When left to chance, the thoughts usually take the form of negative worry about all of the catastrophic possibilities. Such negative images will create anxiety and fear, increasing the probability of undesirable outcomes.

Visualization, on the other hand, is a preplanned, conscious use of the "mind's eye" during a deep, relaxed state to create desirable and fulfilling images of a similar future event. It is a form of what you might call "positive worry." You are about to take an exam and proceed to "worry" about all of the wonderful possibilities that may occur. Such thought patterns will mitigate tension, anxiety and fear, improving the chances for a desirable outcome. During this process, you call into play as many of your five senses as possible to help you formulate clear, vivid images. By so doing, the pictures developed will be more easily interpreted by the central nervous system "as if" they were real. The relaxed state helps to stop the "mind chatter" (distractions) and enables you to focus more sharply on the situation being visualized.

Visualization is not magic or hocus-pocus. It is a learned skill that, when practiced regularly, can change your life from scarcity to abundance by enabling you to focus on what is available to you rather than what you lack. When you "see" limits, they are yours. The idea is to see the positive possibilities and dwell on these by selecting images that complement that path of fulfillment. Of course, visualization will not always provide something that you don't have or are not capable of having; it simply clears the mind to allow the way of nature to unfold. It stops the mind from sabotaging your efforts so you can realize the potential goodness you desire. For example, you could be the most competent person for a job. Nervous, negative self-talk and images will block your efforts to perform up to your capabilities; this hinders your chances of realizing your potential. Visualization works because it sets in motion mental processes that keep you on the road of fulfillment and maximize your chances of positive results. It creates expectations of satisfaction, happiness and joy, and you respond by constructing an environment of people, situations and occurrences that fulfill those expectations.

In addition to this, visualization works because it resembles a dress rehearsal, much like actors getting ready for a stage production. It is a form of practice that increases familiarity with the task, while "working out the kinks" before they have a chance to happen. When the event actually transpires, it is as if you already have been there; it becomes a déjà-vu in this sense.

ESSENTIAL INGREDIENTS TO REMEMBER

Like any skill to be learned, visualization has a number of essential components that increase its effectiveness when included in this process. The following will help to maximize its benefits to you:

BELIEVE IN THE OUTCOME. To have a lackadaisical attitude toward the outcome tells your mind that you really don't care and what you are doing is not important. The stronger your belief, the stronger will be the impression on the brain. Believe and you'll receive.

DESIRE THE OUTCOME. You only attempt to accomplish that which you desire. The obvious example is your desire to live; you program yourself to survive. With visualization, you must have a true desire to have that for which you ask.

VISUALIZE IN THE POSITIVE. When you image an outcome or a process, be sure to state it positively. For example, avoid saying, "I am not tired" or "I am not injured." Instead, state that "I have lots of energy" and "I am healthy and strong." Stating the negative may confuse the mind, and it could pick up on the words "tired" and "injured."

USE THE PRESENT TENSE. You'll notice the above statements are in the present. This helps an image to be more vivid, and the mind then relates to it "as if" it were here and now.

PRECEDE WITH RELAXATION. A calm state of mind is essential to clear, vivid, powerful imagery. You need to silence the "chatter" of the mind in order for the body to get the correct message.

USE ALL YOUR SENSES. The more senses you can call into play, the stronger the imagery and the greater the chance for a successful outcome.

BE PATIENT AND CONSISTENT. Changes take time. Give yourself about three weeks before you see the benefits. They could also happen sooner. Better to visualize five minutes a day for one week than thirty-five minutes once, in seven days. The key is consistency. If you miss a day or two, it doesn't matter that much. Just begin again. Starting to see results and feeling good will provide you with your own motivation, and you will use it more often.

USES AND BENEFITS OF VISUALIZATION

The use of visualization as a tool for spiritual transformation and the restoration of harmony to nature's way is unquestionably effective. I have trained thousands of people over the years, from world-class athletes, to corporate executives, to dancers, musicians, college professors, lawyers, doctors and anyone, of any age, interested in positive life changes and growth, joy and happiness, abundance and fulfillment. The following is a list of some of the specific ways these people have applied this practical tool.

1. To create a peaceful, relaxing period of time during the day.
2. To optimize the chances of a wonderful performance.
3. To help overcome obstacles and self-imposed limits.
4. To reinforce a workable self-image.
5. To cope with fear, anxiety and stress in a more productive way.
6. To help facilitate the process of self-direction.
7. To help increase powers of concentration.
8. To assist in the regulation of blood pressure and heart rate.
9. To facilitate the process of recovery from degenerative diseases.
10. To aid in the restoration of energy.
11. To heighten one's level of joy, happiness and fulfillment.

12. To facilitate the process of changing self-limiting beliefs.

13. To recapture feelings of ideal past performances in order to increase confidence.

14. To cope with frustration and disappointment.

15. To self-regulate mood swings.

This list is far from exhaustive, yet it will give you an idea about how potentially powerful this technique is for creating positive change. Instead of acting according to images, change those that create misalignment with nature, and your life may become more balanced and fulfilled. While you don't have control over much in this life, visualization allows you to take control of your thoughts and views and bring into alignment that which you are able to control.

TO ACT ACCORDINGLY

In the words of author James Allen, "Man is made or unmade by himself; in the armory of thought he forges the weapons by which he destroys himself; he also fashions the tools with which he builds for himself mansions of joy and strength and peace." In your armory or storehouse of visualization, you are capable of forging the tools to create a world of joy and fulfillment.

Since visualization demands a state of relaxation, I will begin with a technique that I have used successfully with most of my clients. Understand that there are many paths to the same light. You should feel free to choose any relaxation tool that enables your mind to approach the ALPHA state, where your brain waves measure approximately seven to fourteen cycles per second (CPS). In this state you are most creative and capable of the most vivid images. It is, for all practical purposes, the dream state. BETA states (fourteen CPS and up) are ineffective for creating vivid images. THETA (four to seven CPS) and DELTA (one to four CPS) states, which occur in deep sleep, are impossible to use for visualization.

The technique is called DEEP ABDOMINAL BREATHING and, with minimal practice, it will create for you a deep relaxed state from which visualization can be used. Naturally, other popular methods such as biofeedback, self-hypnosis, flotation tank therapy, yoga, hot tubs, saunas, music and exercise will have a wonderfully calming effect as well. My preference is the deep breathing technique because it's easy to learn, always accessible, requires no cost or travel time and, when practiced, it will create an alpha state within fifteen seconds. Practice the following for a minimum of ten minutes a day (seven days a week) in a comfortable, quiet place, with your eyes closed. In this state, you will use visualization to enhance your day.

DEEP ABDOMINAL BREATHING EXERCISE:

Breathe only through nostrils (unless clogged); mouth breathing is not relaxing.

Inhale very slowly; as you do, push the abdomen out to its extension as if it were a balloon expanding. As a result, your diaphragm will move downward, allowing full lower extension of lungs.

When abdomen reaches full extension, smoothly draw shoulders back and/or raise head and continue to fill the upper part of lungs. Obtain full extension.

The entire respiratory system has been employed. Now hold breath for FIVE seconds.

Release, exhaling through nostrils slowly. Draw in abdomen, hold for two seconds before resuming next breath.

REPEAT this process for five breaths (more if needed), and as you do, count down 5-4-3-2-1, saying one number on each exhalation. "Feel" yourself getting deeper and deeper into relaxed calmness.

When coming out of the relaxed state, count slowly 1-2-3-4-5. At FIVE, say, "I am relaxed, alert and in fine health." Avoid abrupt transitions, if possible.

As you become more adept at this technique, try using just three deep breaths.

With practice (usually after five or six days of consistent use), you'll be able to create a deep, relaxed state in three breaths. Remember to breathe deeply, but not forcefully, as this may defeat the purpose of relaxing as well as causing you to hyperventilate. Dizziness during the initial practice sessions, although rare, can happen—but no need to worry; simply ease up on the deepness of the breath.

You are now ready to use this tool in conjunction with the following visualization exercises which can be used.

PLACE OF PEACE

In her book, *Creative Visualization*, Shakti Gawain suggests that when you start using mental imagery, the first thing you do is create, in your mind, a place of peace. This sanctuary is your ideal place of inner calm and tranquility. Once there, you can use visualization as you wish. It becomes a place to return to just by closing your eyes and relaxing. It will give you the safety and security you need during times of deep thought. The following exercise is my adaptation of Shakti's enjoyable and powerful exercise.

> Close your eyes. Relax using your personal method. In a comfortable position, imagine yourself in some beautiful, natural environment; let it be any place that appeals to you—perhaps you have actually been there before or maybe you are creating it for the first time.
>
> Is it a meadow, or a mountain home, in a beautiful forest, or on a beach near the ocean? It should feel comfortable and peaceful to you.
>
> Notice all details, sounds, smells and feelings of the environment. Perhaps you would like to have a home there. What would it look like? Arrange the inside in any way you wish. Is there a big deck? If so, see yourself looking over the terrain. You are in control of this script, so create the scene exactly as you would want it.
>
> As you become more familiar with it, your comfort level will increase. Return often whenever the need to be alone and think arises. From this place of peace, you can do all your visual programming. You may

even want to go for a walk on the beach or nearby trails while "vacationing" in this sanctuary.

Allow changes to occur in this environment as the need dictates. Be creative—it's your private place. If you could benefit from a hot tub, install one and "feel" yourself relaxing in the intense heat.

ALPHA CHECK EXERCISE

Here's a quick, fun way to test your level of relaxation and the strength of your images. With your entire body flat on the floor (mat or bed), take five deep breaths and then imagine liquid concrete being poured over the lower parts of your legs: calves, ankles, feet and toes. "See" it, "feel" the texture and temperature, and notice how heavy it is. As it begins to "dry and solidify," notice how the color changes from a dark to a light gray. Take one more deep breath and slowly (do not strain) begin to lift your legs and feel the incredible heaviness of the solid rock. Really get into the image and notice how difficult it is to move your legs. Relax. Now imagine the concrete crumbling to the side, freeing the legs. Count from 1 to 5 and open your eyes. Your legs can now be lifted easily.

If you were still able to lift your legs in spite of the heavy weight of the concrete, you simply need a bit more practice. Lifting your legs simply indicated that your mind wasn't focused on the task as much as it needed to be. Try it again and see if it works. Use this occasionally to check whether you are in the alpha state, because if you are, you will not be able to lift or must struggle to lift your legs.

SCENARIO SWITCH

The purpose of this exercise is to change a negative, stressful and anxious situation to one that is calm, productive, joyful and fulfilling. Perhaps it is a scenario involving someone who's difficult to be around, an impending job interview, or a speech or presentation to a large group of people. Whatever the scene, visualization will enable you to turn things around.

A) Create, in a relaxed state, the negative, counter-productive situation with all of the details exactly as they have been in the past or could be in the future. "Experience" every aspect of the scene and get in touch with the accompanying feelings. When you get anxious...STOP!

B) Now, re-create the same scene except, this time, design it in such a way that it works out exactly the way you would want. "See" the other people reacting to you in the most positive way. Imagine wonderful harmony and joy resulting from this "new" scenario. Experience a calmness and fulfillment that goes beyond your greatest dream. Once you obtain a clear picture of this scene, forget the negative and practice the new, productive one on a regular basis. It then becomes a strong possibility that you will act according to this new scenario when the situation presents itself at some future date.

TRANSFORMATION INSIDE-OUT

Disharmony and imbalance with nature and the world around us occur when we disregard ourselves. To begin to have a positive effect on our universe, we need to begin within; it is an inside-out journey. Chapter Five on self-love will go into more detail, but for now, the following visualization exercise will help you to create a more harmonious inner world to be then mirrored by your outer environment.

In a relaxed alpha state, go to your place of peace and "see" yourself exactly the way you want to be. You are the architect of your world, the director and actor.

Begin by "seeing" your physical self exactly the way you want it to be: strong, beautiful, energetic, vital. How does it feel? Next, "see" yourself in wonderful, comfortable clothing, the kind that makes you feel confident and relaxed. You wear clothes so well. "Feel" the personal power within you. You are emotionally balanced, spiritually grounded and peaceful. You are creating harmony in your world and the world around you.

Experience wonderfully creative outlets through work or other sources. You are receiving an abundance of recognition and support for all that you do. Financial feedback is comfortable and appropriate.

You live in a home that matches your lifestyle, values and interests. You have created an environment that gives you all the love and comfort that you deserve.

Notice the people in your life; they are warm, kind and generous, and they reflect the world you have created. "Feel" the tremendous amount of love and joy that they offer and you accept.

Tell yourself that this is a wonderful world and that you deserve to have a most joyful, fulfilling life. There is enough good for everyone, and you will do what you can to see that this good is multiplied for all.

Repeat this exercise each day for three weeks. As you touch upon all of the above areas, be sure to take the time to actually imagine "as if" it were so. Notice how your relationship to yourself and your world transforms.

WARM RAY OF SUNSHINE

The object of this exercise is to help focus the image of warm, golden light upon your entire being to create a sense of wellness, health and overall physical transformation. Taking care of your body, being vibrant, is an important component of feeling joy and fulfillment.

While deeply relaxed, with eyes closed, imagine a strong, radiant yellow beam of sunlight entering the top of your head. "See" and "feel" it permeate your skull, neck, shoulders, move out your arms to your finger tips, into your chest cavity, and continue to flow throughout your entire body, down to the very last cell.

Notice how it nourishes and nurtures each molecule, bringing with it enormous health, beauty, vibrance and energy. "See" yourself being transformed into a radiant being, full of joy and satisfaction.

Affirmation: "I now do everything that needs to be done to create a most wonderful being. From this moment, I avoid partaking in any substances that will not contribute to my overall health and happiness. I am relaxed, calm and am getting better every day in every way."

Creative visualization is limited only by your imagination. You should feel free to use it in any way that will contribute to a more unlimited, fulfilling life. Its power lies in its ability to align you, immediately, to the laws of nature, once you have created the awareness of such principles. With respect to this, a few words of caution are in order.

First, visualization is only effective when used for the good of all. You should not visualize harm coming to others. For example, rather than seeing others blowing an opportunity, imagine yourself performing well; or, perhaps everyone can do well since there's enough to go around in our abundant world.

Second, what you visualize may not materialize. Rather than criticize the technique, understand the law of nature that says things happen for a reason, even if that reason doesn't immediately make sense. Sometimes your desires are not in your best interests. I remember how devastated I felt being turned down for a job I really wanted. I prepared visually for the interview and came up short. Two weeks later, I was offered a stunning position elsewhere, one that would not have been available to me had I gotten the first job. Such an outcome was a blessing in disguise. So, go with the flow; hold on to your dreams, but lightly. Understand that once you've optimized your chances for your dream, you must be willing to let go if nature sees it in a different light. To insist upon the illusion of control in such situations is to create possible disharmony, frustration, havoc and pain.

Third, visualization was not meant to be used in isolation. It can and should be used along with other tools of change and transformation that are available to us. The Simontons' work with childhood cancer, for example, includes other forms of therapy in addition to visualization. To create fulfillment in any situation, do all that is required to realize the best results, and then use visualization or the "movies of your mind" to create the ideal scenario.

This reminds me of a story told by author Bernie

Siegel, M.D., about a man with a disease that would kill him in an hour if he received no help. He ran to the window and shouted, "God, I'm dying; please save me." A deep voice answered, "Don't worry, my son, I will save you." With that, a team of surgeons, a nurse and a social worker entered the room and told him that if he would permit surgery, they could save him in time. He refused because he thought his prayers would suffice. Within the hour, he died and went to heaven. "I thought you were going to save me!" exclaimed the man. "I tried, but you wouldn't let me," replied God. "Why do you think I sent you all those good doctors?"

Visualization, like prayer, has its best results when used in conjunction with other helpful forces. Like the man who sat on a stool in the middle of a field holding a glass while waiting for a cow to back up into his hands, you will go "milkless" unless you tap into all available resources to bring about the fulfillment of your dreams or needs.

With the conclusion of this chapter, you embark upon the beginning of self-transformation using one of the most powerful tools available for the inner journey of fulfillment. Visualization can actually become a way of life, creating positive movement, joy and fulfillment; it is a *modus operandi* for constructing a joyous inner sanctuary. Like the Tao, use it to go with the flow. Put your needs out to the universe, and do what can be done to place yourself in the best position possible. Then wait patiently for nature to determine the way, regardless of where the path may lead or how rocky it may seem. In the process, you will be better able to enjoy the "trip." Don't force something that doesn't want to move; there may be something better for you "waiting on the wings."

Growth and change are inevitable. In the words of author James Allen, "You cannot travel within and stand still without." With visualization, you are writer, director and actor of all your imagined scripts. Enjoy the show!

CHAPTER FOUR

BEYOND LIMITED BELIEFS: THE ULTIMATE ATTITUDE

*The greatest discovery of my generation
is that human beings, by changing the inner
beliefs of their minds, can change the outer
aspects of their lives.*

William James
(American philosopher)

 BELIEFS AND THE WAY OF NATURE

ou have just been reading about the powerful effect of images and vision upon your reality; what you "see" is what you get—in many ways. So it is with beliefs. A principle of nature that has universal application states that beliefs determine the quality of life; what you believe, you receive. Automotive genius Henry Ford once proclaimed that "whether you believe you can or believe you can't, you are probably right."

When I notice the direction my life has taken, I find that what I achieved or failed to achieve was the direct result of my thoughts or beliefs at that time. Such attitudes had an enormous impact upon the way I related to myself and the world around me. Irrational, illogical, limited subjective beliefs were the cause of much frustration, anger, disappointment, fear, anxiety and other forms of emotional upheaval. My life became more stable, joyous and calm when the beliefs came from a more limitless, expansive, objective posture. Fulfillment flourished during those moments. Let me give you an example.

The words "I can't. . ." are usually based on subjective evidence, nothing more. Unless you have tried, you probably cannot formulate a belief as to what you can or can't do. Believing "you can't" will keep you blind to any possibilities of discovering how you can. This is best exemplified by the allegory of "the magic wishing box":

> A middle-aged man had hoped for years that he would meet someone with whom to share his life. Although he wanted this, he didn't really believe it could happen. One day, he mentioned this to a good friend who suggested that he visit a certain palm reader who had tremendous success helping people to create meaningful relationships. He agreed to do it. When he and the palm reader met, she gave him a magic black box and instructed him to write his wish on a piece of tissue paper, deposit it into the box, and a new person would come into his life. He followed the directions and, shortly thereafter, he met the most incredible woman, fell in love and married her six months later. He went back to the palm reader to share his joy and thank her for the magic box, asking her how it worked. She quickly explained: "There's no such thing as a magic box; the magic is in believing."

You see, believing it was possible activated the psychological processes of motivation, commitment and observation, which helped to create a heightened awareness of the environment and to place him in position to act accordingly. For years, the failure to believe in such possibilities enabled him to choose paths that limited his potential.

This principle of nature, the way that beliefs become reality, can be demonstrated in the following way:

> Have a friend sit in a chair. Then ask this person to stand and reach for the ceiling, as high as possible. Tell the person to reach another three inches. Stretching or getting up on the toes usually facilitates this; let him figure it out. Now say, "Give me two more inches," to which he'll reply, "That's ridiculous, impossible...no way." (If not out loud, then certainly to himself.) Finally, you ask for two more inches. At this point he thinks you're totally crazy. Have him be seated and ask him for comments about what was going on in his mind.

Basically, the reply will indicate a belief that states, it was an impossibility. Once he states this belief, explain to him that from the moment he believed "no way," he chose a path that limited the chances for achieving the goal. He became oblivious to the options, one of which, in this case, was to stand on the chair (or to express this as a solution).

The lesson: Say "I can" until you have explored all possibilities. Judging whether something is possible or not, using subjective beliefs (beliefs with no concrete evidence), is bound to inflict serious limitations upon a situation. This relates to all aspects of life, be it at home, on the job, solving a problem, completing a project or beginning a new relationship.

Misalignment with the law of belief—what you believe, you receive—takes place when you disregard its power and refuse to either become aware of or examine those beliefs that, because of their irrational, limiting nature, cause turbulence throughout life.

Where do these subjective, irrational beliefs originate? As you discovered in Chapter Two about the beginnings of limits, you learn at an early age to cherish certain beliefs as true. They become part of the unconscious network of sloppy thought patterns and, as a result, are rarely questioned; you just assume that "things are that way." Because you can't examine that which you are unaware of, you are unlikely to be able to transcend it.

Most of these beliefs are passed on to you by some authority figure—parent, teacher, doctor, neighbor—which gives them a sense of exactness, trueness or validity. How many of us take the advice of that ubiquitous bumper sticker: "QUESTION AUTHORITY"? Had I done so in my earlier years, life's road would have been much smoother. Just question; you don't need to defy, unless what is being said makes no sense. Consider the example of the so-called significant "expert" medical belief in the early 1950s. Over fifty medical journals throughout the world claimed, at that time, that it was humanly impossible to run faster than a four-minute mile. As a result, no one questioned these bastions of knowledge and truth; no one even tried to test the waters—no one, that is, except Roger Bannister. That astute Englishman saw this belief to be utterly ridiculous, an unnecessary limit, one to be transcended. Bannister hurdled the illogical "obstruction" and cruised to a sterling 3:59.4 mile. The real story, however, came following his feat when within the next year and a half, over forty more athletes proceeded to shatter the four-minute barrier. I have a difficult time believing that, all of a sudden, this many runners became significantly faster. What really happened? Could it be that, because of Bannister, no one continued to believe that the task was impossible? Or that this belief changed the paths that others were then able to choose?

As long as you say "I can," you will increase the chances of goal realization. To believe otherwise will prevent you from even trying. Someone once told me that getting over a seemingly impossible nine-foot brick wall is simply a matter of believing that it can be done. Such an attitude may enable you to see a loose brick or two that, once removed, will facilitate the process. You won't even look at the wall if

you write off the possibility of hurdling the obstacle. This is
so true that all of life's obstructions, because of our limited
belief system, become formidable tasks, never to be challenged. The following are some examples of limited, irrational beliefs that, if left unexamined, can interfere with your
life becoming unlimited and fulfilled.

> I'm not good enough to...
> It can't be done that way.
> This is not the right time (environment, place,
>   location).
> I don't have enough time, don't know enough or have
>   enough.
> I'm too old, fat, tall, short, skinny, stupid...
> That's only for men, women, crazy people...
> I'm not ready.
> They're so much better prepared than I.
> She/he won't understand.

Such beliefs and attitudes could be referred to as "STINKING
THINKING," a term borrowed from author Dan Millman (The
Warrior Athlete). According to Dan, we get locked into un-
productive, limiting attitudes and rigidly defend them. He
calls this widespread phenomenon, "PSYCHOSCLEROSIS—a
hardening of the attitudes." I totally agree. Such a "disease"
metastasizes to the self-image, the vision we have of our
future, the love we have of self and others, the degree of excellence we are capable of achieving and many other aspects
of self that contribute to our level of fulfillment.

Of course, not all beliefs lack harmony with nature.
Many of us have received positive programming from others
while growing up—messages of love, caring, understanding
and respect as well as beliefs that create joy and a refreshing,
wonderful view of life. However, the concern of this chapter
is to help us become aware of and change those irrational,
subjective beliefs (and we all have them) that create obstacles
to fulfillment. It is conservative to estimate that fifty percent

of our beliefs, stored in our unconscious, work as self-imposed limits. A number of researchers have put that figure up to eighty percent. However, such limiting beliefs can be reprogrammed to create more positive results. All beliefs are learned and, therefore, can be unlearned by replacing them with beliefs that allow for the natural flow of a limitless life. Essentially, changing the program means changing limiting beliefs; this alters your path of choice and, ultimately, your life. The key to the process will be your ability to identify those beliefs that impose limits in order for you to go beyond them. Psychologist John Lilly once said that all "beliefs are limits to be examined and transcended." The following exercises will give you a start in the right direction.

TO ACT ACCORDINGLY

I. NAME THAT 'TUDE—as in ATTITUDE. This is a good place to begin. It's simple and revealing. Assume that any unhappiness or feelings of unfulfillment, tension, anxiety or stress are the result of some attitude or belief that has you "stuck" or limited. For example, I have much stress because of deadlines imposed upon me by a certain editor. Failure to meet this time constraint means that I must be incompetent, not good enough, unprofessional. With regard to these beliefs, I ask the following questions:

How valid is my attitude? If it happened all the time, it might be true, but it happens only occasionally. Therefore, there is not much validity to this attitude.
How would I feel if I changed this belief? Wonderful! I usually meet deadlines; if I don't this time, that's unfortunate, but I'm still a competent professional. Thinking this way releases the pressure and, consequently, I am able to work more effectively and increase the chances for meeting the deadline.

This method can be ineffective when the beliefs are difficult to recognize because they are so ingrained that you are unaware of them as limiting attitudes. They become a habit, "the natural way" for you. Such beliefs are usually irrational and represent a total misalignment from the flow of nature; they create enormous stress and anxiety, and they diminish your chances for fulfillment.

In his book *Humanistic Psychotherapy: The Rational-Emotive Approach*, the well-known psychotherapist, Albert Ellis, creates an awareness of some of our more basic irrational beliefs. He offers a method that helps replace such stress-producing attitudes with ones that are stress-reducing. The system is based on the premise that emotions and feelings are the result not of what happens but of our view or belief about what happens. For example:

A) AN EVENT HAPPENS—Exams are taken and failed.

B) HOW YOU EXPERIENCE IT—While at school you take a test.

C) YOUR INTERPRETATION AND BELIEF—Failure is abominable, it's nasty. If I fail, I'll be devastated.

D) EMOTIONS THAT RESULT FROM THAT BELIEF—Anger, stress, anxiety, fear.

E) PROBABLE OUTCOME—Such feelings will interfere with performance, and failure is a realistic possibility.

Since "C" (your belief) causes "D" (your emotions), change "C," and "D" will also change. In other words, if you view failure as *an opportunity from which to learn*, you may be disappointed by the setback but not completely devastated. You will probably look for ways to apply the new knowledge and happily forge ahead at the next or some future opportunity (more on this in the chapter on COURAGE). Be aware that it is difficult to appreciate life as a teacher when it comes in a form we don't value, such as failure; however, by persevering, we can develop a more positive attitude toward such a setback.

The key to this system is to *make the unconscious beliefs conscious*. As with the Tao, become aware and act accordingly. When you discover an old, limiting belief, you need to change it by aligning it with your present value system.

The following system is suggested by Ellis for working with and changing your irrational, limiting beliefs:

A. RECORD AN EVENT THAT CONCERNS OR TROUBLES YOU

EX: My business proposal was turned down.

B. YOUR RATIONAL VIEW

EX: *I need to be more complete, thorough, and try again.*

YOUR IRRATIONAL VIEW

EX: *I'm incompetent; I'm not good enough for them.*

C. EMOTIONS RESULTING FROM YOUR IRRATIONAL VIEW

EX: *depression, tension, fear, anger*

D. CHANGING YOUR IRRATIONAL VIEW OR BELIEF

Ask yourself: *Where is the objective data that proves that I'm incompetent or not good enough?*
Answer: NONE!

Ask yourself: *What's the worst thing that could happen as a result of "A"?*
Answer: I'll be disappointed but I can learn from this and write a better proposal next time.

Ask yourself: *What is an ALTERNATIVE VIEW?*
Answer: I'm competent, and I make mistakes, but I'm getting better and better each time I try.

Ask yourself: *What ALTERNATIVE EMOTIONS do I feel?*
Answer: I feel relieved, confident, and I anticipate positive results in the future.

You can use this system with any belief you have about yourself or the world that is a major cause of stress, anxiety or unhappiness. (Be aware that some of life's events often bring enormous pain and trouble. In such cases, this format might not be appropriate to meet your needs; it may be more important for you to experience grief, for example, and *work through* the natural emotions this causes so that you will better understand the growth such a powerful emotion brings you.) This tool, remember, is a rational process that I have found works quite well for beliefs and views that are not attached to events of immediate catastrophic proportion. Death, divorce or other types of emotional loss may require that you get in touch with the accompanying feelings prior to acceptance and change.

II. THE 'BUT' STOPS HERE—as in "Yes, I should, but..." This exercise is for all of the "yes, but..." people. The beliefs discussed here represent attitudes that seem to have universal significance; that is, they are powerful, common, irrational beliefs that have an impact on legions of people. They seem to have been popularized many years ago and handed down to each generation. The attitudes are limiting and represent a major misalignment with the way of nature. The idea behind this exercise is to recognize these types of beliefs and change them into attitudes that harmonize with the way the natural process actually unfolds. In other words, no more "yes, buts..." For example; when I tell you to stop berating yourself for the less than perfect job you've done, don't reply: "Yes, I should but I wanted to do it perfectly." It's irrational to believe you can achieve perfection, so stay to the left of your but. Just say, "Yes, I should stop berating myself," and leave it at that. (For more on perfection, see chapter on excellence.)

The following is a list of some of the more universal, irrational, limiting beliefs that will misalign you with "the way things are" in this world. They are extremely common, found in áll walks of life and in all cultures. I experience them every day with clients in my practice. On a separate sheet of paper, change each irrational, limiting belief to a view that is more aligned with natural occurrences:

EX: I MUST BE THOROUGHLY COMPETENT AND ACCOMPLISHED IN EVERYTHING I DO. Nature says that errors and mistakes are inevitable—you can't avoid them. The results of believing that you can always be competent are frustration, self-blame, lowered self-esteem and tremendous disappointment.

CHANGED BELIEF: *I am fallible like everyone else, and I know it's natural to make occasional mistakes; failure is a powerful learning tool.*

I CAN ONLY BE HAPPY AND FULFILLED WHEN I'M WITH OTHERS. Nature says that solitude is a valuable component of self-growth. Creating a balance between being with people and having alone-time is essential. The results of believing that only others can bring you joy are poor self-image, over-dependence and lack of self-confidence.

CHANGED BELIEF: _____

_____

IT IS ABSOLUTELY NECESSARY TO BE LOVED AND APPROVED OF BY EVERYONE. Nature says that enemies (or those who take exception to our beliefs or actions) are the normal outcome of involvement in life. If Christ, Gandhi and Mother Theresa can't be loved by all, who among us can? The attempt to win universal love and approval is probably the greatest cause of unfulfillment; it guarantees unhappiness.

CHANGED BELIEF: _____

_____

I AM AT THE MERCY OF FORCES BEYOND MY CONTROL. Nature says that you have considerable control over your choices, views and interpretations of events as they occur. You are affected by your *views* of circumstances, not by the circumstances themselves. This irrational belief creates feel-

ings of helplessness and victimization. You can learn to understand and then control your emotional responses; you can learn to change your *views* and therefore change *how you respond.*
CHANGED BELIEF:_____

_____

MY SELF-WORTH IS ONLY MEASURED BY MY ACCOMPLISH-MENTS. Nature says that self-worth is based on an appreciation of internal qualities rather than on external achievements. To measure yourself by the outcome of your goals is a sure set-up for self-imposed misery. What you are *inside* is the true measure of your character and worth.
CHANGED BELIEF:_____

_____

I MUST PLEASE OTHERS AND THEN THEY'LL ACCEPT ME. Nature says that acceptance is based upon approval of the "real you." Trying to please others at all times means putting aside your true self. This belief is the result of a low self-image and causes great confusion about who you really are. "People pleasing" will always result in rarely pleasing, or knowing, your true self.
CHANGED BELIEF:_____

_____

LIFE'S HAPPENINGS ARE SUPPOSED TO BE THE WAY I WOULD LIKE THEM TO BE. Nature is the way it is—you can't control the process; you can only go with the flow. Do what you can to help nature along, but if it doesn't turn out the way you hope, there's no point in reacting like a "spoiled child." Evaluate and refocus; learn from each experience. Otherwise, much stress and unnecessary anguish will result. Accept what cannot be immediately changed.
CHANGED BELIEF:_____

PAST EVENTS ARE THE DICTATORS OF PRESENT SITUATIONS. Nature says that the past is the source of your wisdom, provided you are aware of its lessons. The past has power over you *only* if you have not learned from it and made appropriate changes. You decide, at every moment, how to use what you have learned. Believing that you are totally controlled by past events is inappropriate behavior; what you do now with their lessons is what matters.
CHANGED BELIEF:_____

_____

I AM ENTITLED TO A GOOD LIFE WITH NO PAIN. Nature says that pain and emotional upheaval are inevitable; life is not always fair and suffering does occur. However, notice how hurt and pain usually bring about valuable personal growth; "no pain, no gain" is an appropriate aphorism.
CHANGED BELIEF:_____

_____

I FIND IT EASIER TO AVOID, RATHER THAN CONFRONT, DIFFICULT SITUATIONS. Nature says that what you resist will persist. Attempting to avoid uncomfortable situations is futile; they don't go away. Actually, you contribute to the power they have over you by denying their existence. The result is low-grade anxiety, tension and stress over the inevitable. In addition to the situation, the avoidance process itself also causes pain.
CHANGED BELIEF:_____

_____

You probably have accumulated a number of other irrational attitudes in your life. To discover these additional self-limiting beliefs, concentrate on those instances when you experience anxiety, depression, stress, guilt, worry and unhappiness. Oftentimes, the root of such emotions is an irrational set of words that helps to form the beliefs that are

misaligning you with the way of nature. Much of our unfulfillment in life originates with such negative, unproduc-
tive, self-limiting beliefs.

III. BACK TO YOUR FUTURE. Here is a way to use your past
to gain confidence and believe in your future. For example,
your BELIEFS about what is possible in the years to come
are often tainted by a limited imagination. You can't believe
that certain things could be possible; they seem to be too
farfetched. However, as you will learn in the chapter called
VISION, you must act AS IF all were possible in order to activate the psychological processes that will put you in a position for such things to occur. In other words, to help me
assume this "as if" attitude, I "place" myself ten years back into the past and imagine my life as it truly exists today. My
reaction is: "I can't believe it; it's incredible!" The professional, social, athletic, spiritual and financial aspects of my
life today would have seemed totally impossible to me in
that distant past—beyond my imagination. Because this is so,
when I dream today about the future, I now can say, "why
not?" And anyone, at any age, can learn to say, "why not?"
and begin the exciting process of changing his life and going
after his dreams. Remember, your beliefs about what is possible are only limited by your imagination. What you believe
you usually receive. The key is to change your beliefs about
what is possible from scarcity to abundance, from limited
scenarios to expansive ones. Be aware, however, that some of
us have always preferred life to be wonderful, yet it hasn't
unfolded as such. Other variables can and do contribute to
life's passages and your beliefs are one of them. The purpose
behind this section is to control those beliefs.

The following exercise will help you to discover the
working patterns of your life in five-year increments and to
apply that knowledge to your future. Naturally, this will be
restricted by the depth of your experience, but it should indicate to you how what you viewed as "impossible" in years

past has now become your present reality. Why couldn't it happen once again...and again...and again? Notice how difficult it would have been for you before to imagine how things would be as they now are.

Fill in the following "growth grid" with as much relevant information as possible. Compare the past with the present and notice the incredible growth. Amazing, isn't it? This should help you to dream more expansively for the future.

CHANGES

PERSONAL

PRESENT	5 YEARS AGO
10 YEARS AGO	15 YEARS AGO

PROFESSIONAL
      PRESENT   5 YEARS AGO

      10 YEARS AGO   15 YEARS AGO

PHYSICAL
      PRESENT   5 YEARS AGO

      10 YEARS AGO   15 YEARS AGO

EMOTIONAL

      PRESENT   **5 YEARS AGO**

      10 YEARS AGO   **15 YEARS AGO**

SPIRITUAL

      PRESENT   **5 YEARS AGO**

      10 YEARS AGO   **15 YEARS AGO**

For all those instances in the past where you wouldn't have believed that your present situation could be possible, use these same instances NOW to change your limiting beliefs about what is possible for the future. (The chapters on vision and direction will be quite helpful.) Remember, like the child, to believe it's possible until all objective data, not your old belief patterns, prove otherwise. The key to going beyond limited beliefs is to become aware of those beliefs that hinder as well as those that promote growth, expansion and joy, and then to act accordingly. Keep only those beliefs that cooperate with the forces of nature and transcend all the rest. Much of our unfulfillment is the result of defending and holding on to beliefs that oppose the natural flow of life. Once you understand this, you gain personal power, the power to choose and view your world in a more constructive, positive fashion. To be unlimited, remember that, like an umbrella, the mind works best when opened. Fixed and rigid belief systems create disharmony with a life that is ever-changing. Like the child, open your heart and be receptive to the changes. Act upon the world as it is, not as you think it should be.

Inflexibility of belief systems is a sure path to basic unhappiness and unfulfillment. In R. L. Wing's translation of the *Tao Te Ching*, it is said that,

Those who are firm and inflexible
are in harmony with dying.
Those who are yielding and receptive
are in harmony with living.

To live life to its fullest, examine those beliefs that are no longer applicable or appropriate to your present life and let go, yield and go with the flow...with the way things are...the way of nature. You can choose to adopt new, more appropriate beliefs and attitudes that will support you on your inner journey. In a state of deep relaxation, visualize and repeat often: "I am now ready to release all beliefs and attitudes that are obstacles to my path of fulfillment."

Coming full circle, let me repeat that you are only limited by what you THINK you can or can't do. Nature's way dictates that your reality is directly related to the strength of those beliefs. When I was seventeen years old, an elderly neighbor gave me an anonymous poem. I have referred to it often throughout my life and share it with you now.

Think

If you THINK you are beaten, you are.
If you THINK you dare not, you don't.
If you like to win, but THINK you can't,
It is almost certain you won't!

If you THINK you'll lose, you've lost,
For out in the world we find,
Success begins with a person's WILL—
It's all in the state of MIND.

If you THINK you're outclassed, you are.
You've got to THINK high to rise.
You've got to be sure of yourself before
You can ever win a prize.

Life's battles don't always go
To the stronger or faster one,
But sooner or later the one who wins
is the one who THINKS he can!

CHAPTER FIVE

BEYOND LIMITED SELF-LOVE: THE ULTIMATE NEED

I wouldn't want to be part of an organization that would have me as a member.

Groucho Marx

SELF-LOVE AND THE WAY OF NATURE

Surely you have noticed how some days go quite well, while others seem to slowly deteriorate from the moment your feet hit the floor after that intrusive alarm shocks you awake. Many variables could account for such diverse directions yet, more than likely, how you feel about and relate to your SELF is a powerful determining factor in how your day unfolds. According to the laws of nature, all of your relationships with the world are mirrors of your relationship with yourself. If you are in harmony and aligned with yourself, the chances are great that you will experience harmony, joy and fulfillment with your outer world. I know most of the problems in my life occur when my love of self is scarce, when it seems to disintegrate or temporarily disappear. I notice that this is also true for so many others whose problems are directly related to their inability or unwillingness to love themselves. We seem to fight, alter or avoid who we basically are through unacceptance and disapproval of self. We sit in constant judgment of ourselves, ready to be tried, convicted and hung at dawn. In the words of the cartoon character Pogo, "We have met the enemy and they are us."

Misalignment with this law of mirrors is the cause of so many of the problems we experience in daily life, limiting our chances for joy, health and happiness. How you relate to yourself determines how and what you eat, the amount of sleep you get, whether or not you wear seatbelts, how much exercise you get and whether you drink alcohol, smoke or take drugs. And how you treat yourself directly affects the outcome of relationship difficulties, professional upheaval, financial concerns, stress, anxiety, depression and illness, all of which seem to originate from a basic lack, or scarcity, of self-love. Self-love is simply your own approval of the way you are; in a sense, it's "turning on to yourself," creating enough self-abundance so that you have plenty to give to other people and situations. Self-love means being uncritical, understanding and kind to yourself so that you can relate to the world with the same compassion. If you are happy with you, if your relationship with the outer world works, then your life will be filled with joy.

I can honestly say that ninety percent of those coming to me for psychotherapy have difficulties resulting from their self-unacceptance or lack of self-love. Other professional colleagues seem to agree. Noted author Bernie Siegel, M.D., in his wonderful book about self-healing called *Love*,

Medicine and Miracles, tells of a woman with breast cancer who came to him and said, "I guess you're going to tell me to stop smoking." Siegel replied, "No, but I'm going to tell you to love yourself. Then you'll stop."

I used a similar approach with an obese young man who desperately tried to shed pounds rather than risk continued cardiac problems. Yet, all diet interventions failed to help him; scare tactics from doctors went nowhere. He came to me, having been told his problem was of deep psychological origin, one with heavy emotional overtones. After we got to know each other somewhat better, I asked him when he was going to begin to love himself. A bit confused by this approach, he wondered how that could matter. "If you love yourself," I said, "why do you continue to abuse your body?" In time, he made the connection and began to lose weight. With a journey of self-love and appreciation, he began to view life differently and relate to others in less destructive ways. More importantly, his self-approval and self-acceptance allowed change to occur with less friction and more internal harmony. It is an interesting paradox of life that change will take place only where acceptance is experienced. Self-love put him in position, for the first time, to work with other forms of therapy (visualization, nutrition and exercise) with the hope and confidence that it could be done. His work was the "labor of love" in its purest sense.

Understanding the law of mirrors and how harmony with yourself creates harmony and fulfillment in your life is crucial. You need self-love because:

> You can't receive love from others if you can't love yourself. If someone says, "I love you," your brain replies, "I don't deserve it." To paraphrase the quote by Groucho Marx, how could *you* be part of an organization that would have you as a member? You don't deserve it. Then again, *they* can't be all that great if they invited a nothing like you.
>
> You can't give love to others if you can't love yourself. Giving love to others creates the fear that you'll run

dry. It's the fear of scarcity (SCARE-CITY, remember?). The more I give away, the less I'll have. Of course, nothing could be further from the truth when it comes to love. What you give out in love comes back to you a thousand-fold.

You'll be controlled by negative emotions that stem from the lack, or scarcity, of self-love. For example, defensiveness, anger, fear and depression germinate in loveless soil.

You'll be controlled by limiting, negative thought patterns about yourself; lack of self-love permits you to accept such beliefs as true, never to be questioned or changed.

With self-love, you can "do it all." I remember a cartoon of a shiny steam locomotive with a smile on its face as it hauled one hundred cars up a steep hill. It proudly exclaimed, "Anything is possible when you feel good about your self."

So it becomes clear, once again, that being aligned with nature's way can provide harmony with and joy in the world, allowing you to go beyond your limited self-love and experience fulfillment. Your world is a mirror of yourself. In his book, *The Tao of Leadership,* John Heider talks about "how things work" using the ripple effect metaphor. Your influence in the world must start with you. Get yourself on the move and the movement will ripple outward. He states that "all growth spreads outward from a fertile and potent nucleus." You are that nucleus. You can't help but influence others, and it seems clear that the effect you create will be determined by how you relate to or care for yourself. To continue to judge, criticize, blame or abuse yourself will result in chaos and disharmony.

Notice the reactions of a typical three-year-old child. If scolded, criticized and humiliated for an accident, he or she will either clam up, become timid and shy, or "act out" in destructive ways. Treat the same child, under the same circumstances, with tender, loving care, understanding and kindness, and the child will blossom with self-love and

enormous creative potential. You and I, as adults, are no different. We still have within us much of that curious, loving,
energetic three-year-old. Why do we insist upon creating a
scarcity of self-love through behaviors that ultimately destroy
our physical, mental and emotional selves? The key to
eliminating such chaos in your life and creating the joy and
fulfillment you deserve is to begin to genuinely love yourself.
Through praise, acceptance, approval and other positive self-
strokes, you will become aligned and balanced with yourself
and your immediate relationships, with your community,
country and world.

TO ACT ACCORDINGLY

How do I find self-love when I feel
worthless? I don't deserve it. I've been
beating up on myself for years. I'm not OK!
If my friends ever treated me the way I treat
myself, that would be the end. I'd never
talk to them again.

Although these words ring true for many of us, they are from
an actual dialogue during a recent therapy session with one
of my clients. I told the woman, "I'm not OK, you're not OK
and that's OK," thinking that self-acceptance would be a
logical place to start; after all, even therapists are not always
OK, and maybe we can help each other. Her reply: "It's OK
for others to not be OK, but that's not OK for me." I began to
realize that I was working with a perfectionist who could
now beat up on herself for not being OK—the ultimate
"double whammy." As it is for so many of us, lack of self-love
and acceptance had become deeply ingrained from years of
negative self-talk and abuse. She had brainwashed herself into believing that "she can't live up" or "doesn't deserve" or is
totally worthless. Such brainwashing techniques are no less
effective when used by advertisers, particularly with TV
commercials. Hear something often enough and you begin to
believe it. The subliminal mind dictates much of our

behavior; it is in this part of the brain that brainwashing has its greatest effect.

Before my client left for the day, I asked her to do some homework. Perhaps this would be a good place for all of us to begin. If brainwashing works, why not put it to positive use? I asked her to compose four or five messages, phrases, statements and quips that would express the way she would love to view herself, even if she didn't believe them to be true. She came up with the following, after much prompting and encouragement:

1. I, (name), am a wonderfully unique, valuable woman.
2. I love myself, I think I'm grand, I lie in bed and hold my hand.
3. I'm neat and can't be beat!
4. I like who I am and I'm free to be me.
5. I love my life and deserve all that's good.

I proceeded to instruct her to write these statements on large index cards, using magic marker pens, and to place them on the refrigerator door, for example, or the dashboard of her car, the bathroom mirror, in her date book, next to her bed and any other place where, daily, she could see them and recite them over and over again. I encouraged her to repeat them during her deep, relaxed state of visualization and to image herself just as she had described her ideal self above. She needed to follow the routine for eight weeks. This, coupled with a few of the following strategies, began to create wonderful changes in her. The old negative self began to fade and be replaced by more constructive patterns of behavior. Friends who saw her self-love cards began to give her the strokes she deserved; they supported her journey, and this mushroomed into a burst of incredible love throughout every area of her life. She was creating a new world that, in the true course of nature, was a mirror of herself. This flash-card exercise took complete advantage of the lessons I've discussed in Chapters Three and Four: learning to create harmony by going beyond limited self-love.

The following tools and strategies can be used individually or in combination with each other to help you create a more powerful, unlimited sense of self-love. They are meant to be guidelines, not rigid formulas to which one must adhere. Flexibility and harmony are important components of the Tao. This needs to be remembered during the application of such techniques. Be creative and vary these suggestions so they can blend naturally with your world. (This advice holds true for all the exercises in this book.)

GIFT OF LOVE

One of the most frequently asked questions from those of us who seem to have a scarce amount of self-love is: "How do I learn to love myself when there's nothing there to love?" It's the *Catch-22* of the love cycle. When you feel worthless, you can't love yourself; if you can't love yourself, you feel worthless. The answer to this dilemma is, paradoxically, simple: You must not wait for love; you must give it in order for it to be yours.

You might logically ask, "How can I give what I don't have?" To which I reply, "You have it, you just don't see it." What you *do* see, you are afraid to give away at the risk of coming up empty-handed. So many of us think love is a commodity like money or food; spend it or give it away and it's gone. We must hoard it, save it for a rainy day so we don't get caught short. That's not so. Love is one of the few things in life that increases exponentially when shared. Give and receive. Receive and believe—believe that you are deserving of love and incorporate that feedback with the index card statements of self-love. This will create powerful changes in a mind-set devoid of such caring.

So, don't wait for love; give it. For the following seven days, give love once each day and notice how you begin to feel good about yourself. *Notice that!*

This list should be a guide to some of the ways to share love.

1. Ask someone how you can help, and follow through.

2. Give of your valuable time and really listen to someone.

3. Volunteer for a worthwhile cause, within or outside the home.

4. Give words of love, encouragement or praise to others.

5. Call or write to someone with no motive other than love and caring.

6. Offer to babysit for a friend's children—for free. This is a powerful way to give and receive from many people.

7. Take on unwanted projects at home or at work.

8. Send flowers or give a gift for no reason other than love.

9. Cook dinner for a friend when they least expect it.

10. And, to see the humor in it all, if you drive on a toll road or bridge, try paying for the car in line behind you and tell the collector, in turn, to ask them to do it for someone else in the future.

The key to success using these suggestions is to be sure you only consider doing them *unconditionally*. In the words of the SAMURAI WARRIOR: "Expect nothing; be ready for anything." Giving, in this way, is a catalyst for much joy and fulfillment, as well as self-love.

TAKING CARE OF NUMBER ONE

One of the manifestations of limited self-love is self-neglect. You tend to avoid taking care of yourself by abusing your body, mind and spirit. Such abuse is a symptom of the greater, more fundamental problem of not loving yourself. For example, people who have an abundance of self-love do not smoke. Since smoking destroys the body, why would someone who truly loved himself continue to smoke?

The following is a list of those areas of life that we tend to neglect out of a scarcity of self-love. Read how to create an abundance of love. Fill in the blank lines indicating how you may be self-neglectful. Record how you plan to change one of these areas that blends with life as you now experience it.

BODY
Abundance: Because I love myself, I ingest nourishing foods and beverages; get plenty of sleep and rest; exercise frequently; avoid harmful drugs; use seatbelts; floss and brush my teeth; groom my hair.
Scarcity: I neglect my body by _____
_____
_____

I plan to change by _____
_____

MIND-SPIRIT
Abundance: Because I love myself, I use meditation and relaxation techniques on a consistent basis; read thought-provoking books of spiritual value; trust myself and use my intuition more often (see chapter on intuition). I am more self-accepting through a sense of humor, not taking myself so seriously.
Scarcity: I neglect my mind-spirit by _____
_____

I plan to change by _____
_____

ENVIRONMENT
Abundance: Because I love myself, I live in a geographic area of my choice. I create a wonderful, comfortable home with much love and thought given to each room. I provide time and space for solitude as well as for being together with family and friends.
Scarcity: I neglect my environment by _____
_____

I plan to change by _____
_____

WORK-JOB-PROFESSION

Abundance: Because I love myself, I choose work I thoroughly enjoy. The work is aligned with my interests, talents and abilities. At work I choose to surround myself with positive, creative people. I earn enough money to create what I need in life.

Scarcity: I neglect my work by _____

_____

I plan to change by _____

_____

RELATIONSHIPS

Abundance: Because I love myself, I create relationships that are alive and free. Friends love and nurture me as I do them. Intimacy is a risk I am willing to take in order to increase my chances for joy and fulfillment. I seek others with whom to share my life.

Scarcity: I neglect relationships by _____

_____

I plan to change by _____

_____

STICKS, STONES AND WORDS...

I recall, as a young boy, telling others that sticks and stones may break my bones but words will never harm me. But they did; and they continue to hurt in powerful ways.

For example, how many of you remember the kid on the block named "Shorty"? He was the one who always acted out and caused trouble just to get attention, as negative as it was. Or how about "fat, fat the water rat." She grew up with a tremendous handicap and became a social outcast. And then there was "Four-Eyes"; his self-image never had a chance.

Kids can be heartless; yet as they mature, they seem to outgrow the need to criticize and hurt others. They become more accepting, except when it comes to themselves. The vicious, negative self-talk continues to devastate its victim. Such "scarcity-of-self-love" statements, coupled with an abundance of words that pierce one's heart, create an environment where not even the hardiest of people can survive unscathed.

You are like a flower; you grow and blossom when placed in a warm, nurturing environment, free of words that choke off your life's sources. You need to cultivate the life-giving soil of your mind so that it becomes a fertile breeding ground for the new language of self-love. This takes time and patience, as would be the case for any new seedling being planted. Your garden must be weeded to remove the negative, destructive words that inhibit and limit your growth.

The purpose of this next exercise is to become more conscious of the harmful "self-love-reducing" words you use and to substitute them with ones that are "self-love-producing."

SELF-LOVE-REDUCING WORDS   **SELF-LOVE-PRODUCING WORDS**

1.
2.
3.
4.
5.
6.
7.
8.
9.
10.

Fill in the left-hand column with words that are self-abusive, destructive, judgmental and critical. You may need to take your time to complete the list, perhaps a week, and notice how you use such language. When the list is complete, see the folly in each statement that's totally subjective, and change it to one that is more rational, objective and true. Write that new statement under "Self-Love-Producing

Words." For example, I make a mistake and say, "I'm such a jerk." The truth is I made an error, as we all do, and have lots of evidence to prove I'm competent and capable. Therefore, I'll change the initial subjective statement to: "I make mistakes and I'm still competent."

Try to list those words that have plagued you for quite some time, words that permit you to "beat up" on yourself and make you feel undeserving. Creating self-love statements won't bring about instant change. The mind is like the child whose parents want to change his or her eating habits. At first, the child rebels and resists. However, if the parents are fair and firm, change will occur. Your mind will resist the new language yet, in time, will accept it as the truth, and it will become the new habit.

A LOVE STORY...
In a deep, relaxed alpha state, eyes closed, create the most wonderful story of self-love in your mind. Remember that by so doing, the world will mirror your picture, and all will benefit from the way you feel. "See" yourself standing before a full-length mirror, staring into your eyes. Appreciate the way you look; you're unique and wonderful. You enjoy yourself with all of your idiosyncracies. "Tell" yourself how much trust and respect you have for yourself and that others feel the same. Let this vibrate throughout your whole body.

Now, begin to "walk" over to the door and leave the house. Drive or walk to a wonderfully supportive friend's house; the two of you are going out for a special dinner at your favorite restaurant. "Hear" the conversation; it's meaningful, compassionate and filled with humor. It is terrific how things unfold, particularly how you feel about yourself in relation to everything around you. Notice how much you love yourself and how this reflects upon all that is happening.

At this point, finish the scenario according to how you would like it to flow, being sure to remain in harmony with all that you do. Remember and repeat, "My relationships with the world are a mirror of my relationship with myself." This is the law of nature, the way things are.

It is crucial to remind ourselves that our focus with self-love is not one of selfishness, with the goal of placing ourselves beyond others on some "goodness" rating scale. Self-love is a selfless process that puts you in position to give without the fear of scarcity. People who come from "inner debt" are truly selfish because they have an incessant need to take from others in order to "fill up" this empty tank. Going beyond limited self-love creates an inner-abundance of joy and that permeates your entire universe. If you are willing to view your quest as a way of creating a better world, it is truly a selfless act. In the process, a balance is created; as you begin to give, so will you receive. Such balance is truly within the spirit of the Tao; true self-interest teaches selflessness. John Heider, in his book *The Tao of Leadership*, talks about this balance: "Placing the well-being of all above the well-being of self," paradoxically, enhances the self.

Be aware that the chapters on personal power and affirmations will serve as natural extensions and complements to this one on self-love. You may wish to utilize them individually or blend them as a harmonious unit.

CHAPTER SIX

BEYOND LIMITED POWER: THE ULTIMATE PERSONAL IMAGE

I believe that knowing oneself is the most important thing a human being can do for himself. How can one know oneself? By learning to act not as one should, but as one does.

Moshe Feldenkrais

Watching a two-year-old trying to force a rectangular object into a triangular hole creates a picture of one of life's more interesting metaphysical lessons. In a short time, that child will learn that everything has its place; the laws of nature, once again, cannot be fooled. Align the figure with the appropriate opening and things work out; so it is with people. Align your life with who you are, and harmony and joy will emerge. You, too, have your place.

Yet notice how quickly this lesson is forgotten. The actions, activities and behavior of many of us soon become misaligned with who we really are. We force our round bodies into square jobs or octagonal relationships, only to become miserably unhappy and unfulfilled. Like all things in nature, you have a place, an appropriate environment based upon who and what you are. Cactus doesn't do well in Alaska; polar bears in the Amazon? Hardly! Most things in nature know who they are and where they belong, and live accordingly. We, on the other hand, lose track of our inner nature and become misaligned with what works best for us. Our personal image about who we are becomes distorted as we forget how to "fit into" the grand design of nature. This image may become inflated or deflated, depending upon how far off course we get. In either case, the image is inaccurate, and since we act according to our self-image ninety percent of the time, we will experience the constant frustration of the two-year-old child playing with objects as we try to "squeeze into" a world where we can't fit.

With this in mind, nature's law of personal power becomes a manifestation of the Tao, the way things are. According to this law, power is established when you become conscious of who you really are and act accordingly. To do otherwise is to cause disharmony with the inner self, and problems will surely arise. How many of us are presently experiencing problems in life because we are in a job situation that's "not us"? Or, perhaps, not knowing who we really are placed us in relationships that did not work. This happens to be the downfall of many who marry young. They finally get to know themselves and, one day, awaken to ask, "Why am I with this person? We don't blend." I can truthfully say that my most unhappy years have been when I followed what I thought I "should" do rather than what I wanted to do; those "shoulds" were based on a misreading of the real me. When I began to know, appreciate and accept the person I am, life became much more meaningful and fulfilling.

Like the Tao, you, too, are a natural process: You grow, blossom and unfold according to the same principles of nature. Experiencing inner power results from nurturing the inner, true, realistic self and acting not as you should but *as you do*. Elephants may think they should fly but they can't. They do many other things quite well. I can't help but remember the story of a short high school basketball player; when he realized he was really a gymnast, he wasn't "short" any longer.

As Moshe Feldenkrais stated in the introductory chapter quote, knowing yourself is the most important thing you can do for yourself. However, for most of us, our self-image often reflects something we are not, and this is when the trouble begins. Many of us remain unconscious about who we really are. Sometimes we establish an inflated, unrealistic portrait based on that image, and so we experience frustration. We can't live up to the picture we've created about ourselves. Measuring self-worth on the basis of not achieving these unrealistic goals creates tremendous inner stress, chaos, disappointment and general unhappiness. On the other hand, a deflated concept of self will force us to underestimate our abilities and establish unnecessary limits. Our potential will be blocked and, as a result, so will the opportunity for joy and fulfillment. Much of the fulfillment we experience in this life is attached to potential realization. When this potential is limited because the image or concept of self is distorted, then fulfillment diminishes as well. The key to the principles of unlimited personal power, therefore, is to find out who you really are and to begin to act in ways that complement the real you—ways that work best with what you've got.

How do you lose touch with the real you? How do you become misaligned with nature's law of personal power and fail to recognize the true value of self?

As with the subject of attitudes discussed in Chapter Four, self-images are beliefs, learned in childhood from our environment. For example, a young boy was referred to me recently because he was "acting out" uncontrollably in school. Teachers remarked that he had a low self-concept and craved attention and approval. When his mom came to the office to discuss the problem, I asked where her son was. She replied, "He's out in the car; I'll get him." The next words I heard were, "Hey, Shorty, you can come in now." There it was: the constant, daily reminder of who and what he is. I, too, would act out if "Shorty" were my name. Such an albatross becomes a heavy cross to bear for any child. With just a change of his name and encouragement from his teachers, Jackie became an angel.

The following poem by Dorothy Law Nolte gives us an indication of how we evolve:

> If children live with criticism, they learn to condemn.
> If children live with hostility, they learn to fight.
> If children live with ridicule, they learn to be shy.
> If children live with shame, they learn to feel guilty.
> If children live with tolerance, they learn to be patient.
> If children live with encouragement, they learn confidence.
> If children live with praise, they learn to appreciate.
> If children live with fairness, they learn justice.
> If children live with security, they learn to have faith.
> If children live with approval, they learn to like themselves.
> If children live with acceptance and friendship, they learn to find love in the world.

The child who is chastised for spilling milk on the new rug, told that he is a clumsy ox and then punished for the rest of the evening, will learn to internalize this criticism if it's repeated often enough. Such a distorted image will handicap his potential; he will become limited because his image of self dictates that this is so. He may get the picture that he's incompetent and awkward; taking chances or risks in the future will be minimized out of fear of possible rejection or criticism. Here's the way such misalignment affects one's potential:

> **GOAL:** To be interviewed for a certain job
>
> Distorted Self-Image: "I'm not a person who gets what I want."
>
> "I'm not good enough."
>
> Mind's Interpretation: "I'll never get the job."
>
> "I'll probably look ridiculous."
>
> Likely Outcome: Will not go to interview, or
>
> Will go but fail because of anxiety and fright.

As you can see, potential is greatly influenced by concepts of self. Although you may have established this image over the years, there is no reason to continue lugging around negative portraits. They can be changed by getting in touch with the real you and acting accordingly. *You are never too old to alter your image for a wider, more fulfilled life.*

Creating a realistic self-image, one that blends with the real you, will not give you what you don't have or deserve. It will, however, enable you to release and utilize those talents, abilities and traits you already possess. It will also improve your sense of self-worth and confidence which, working together, will put you in position to experience positive growth and change. Discovering this "true" self will put an end to underestimating the magnitude of the gifts you have within. When you recognize and appreciate your own value, you will achieve a more fulfilling existence. Understand, however, that this may take some time; but the effort is worth it. Benjamin Hoff, in *The Tao of Pooh*, reminds us of the Chinese story of the stonecutter, which I have adapted here to illustrate this point. The stonecutter was unappreciative of his position in life; seeing a wealthy merchant, he wished he could be such.

When he became one, he realized that with all
this power, he still had to bow before the
king; of course, he now wished to be king.
And so it was, until he noticed how much the
sun could make him uncomfortable with its
heat. How powerful the sun is, he thought,
so he became the sun until the cloud showed
its power by covering up the sun. He then
became the powerful cloud until, one day, the
mighty wind pushed him around. He then
became the wind, which could do all except
blow the powerful stone. He became the
stone, more powerful than anything on earth.
As he stood proudly in the wind, he asked
what could be more powerful than a stone? As
he looked down, he saw a stonecutter,
pounding him with a chisel.

We must begin to become aware of our personal value,
believe in it and take risks to cultivate that power. We have,
within us, all that is needed to realize a fulfilling existence.
We have simply to notice and behave accordingly.

The tools, strategies and exercises that follow will
enable you to become more aware of who you really are and
who you potentially can be as a result of what you already
have within. An appreciation of this self will encourage action and behavior in this direction.

It may be helpful to notice that the work you do with
the images and beliefs about self in the following section
will blend beautifully with the tools learned in Chapters
Three, Four and Five. Using them together will produce
powerful results.

TO ACT ACCORDINGLY

As the law of nature states, your chances for fulfillment and
happiness increase when you establish personal power by
becoming conscious of who you really are and acting accordingly. To act according to this principle, be aware that you
will discover aspects of your real self that you don't like.
That's as natural as the law itself. There's no need to run

away from these negative sides; no one is perfect and we all have innate flaws. What needs to be done in most areas is to *direct your weaknesses to a different path* than you did in the past. The debit becomes a credit when you begin to see how that shortcoming in some situations is a strength in others. For example, sometimes my directness can be interpreted as rudeness; however, I remain aware of the benefits of this truthfulness while I work on becoming less rude.

Also, your "true self" should not become a self-imposed limit, never to be changed. Yes, it's true you are a certain basic way; however, be aware that you can embellish and improve upon who you "really" are and become even more dynamic. For example, as one of the following exercises will show, if you discover someone's traits that you admire or skills you'd like to internalize, they are available to you. Simply noticing such things in others means that they probably exist within you, albeit in a dormant state. You need only awaken them.

PATHS TO PERSONAL POWER

Mind-Body Exploration. This strategy is becoming more popular as people begin to discover themselves through challenging physical paths. Although it didn't start out to be a journey of self-exploration, my experiences with long-distance running have been powerful lessons in inner discovery. Racing marathons (26.2 miles) and pushing myself "to the max" taught me to be with myself amid the pressures of competition. I learned the meaning of mind-body harmony as I was forced to blend into a cohesive unit. Through running, I have had many opportunities to explore frightening, threatening aspects of my immediate world. I essentially became familiar with how I work and deal with unpredictable circumstances. The lessons have permeated deep within my essence and act as a guide to who I am and how I choose to behave. Because of my running experience, I accomplished things I never thought I could do; transcendence in other aspects of life became possible. All of this and more resulted from the simple desire to "get in shape" and shed a few pounds.

I am at a loss for words to explain (without proselytizing) the effects of such physical experiences upon one's quest for inner understanding. And running need not be the only beam to the light. I have heard similar reactions from people involved in martial arts such as aikido, cross-country skiing, swimming, wilderness hiking, sky diving and mountain climbing, to name but a few. Most who report such experiences agree that physical prowess, talent or ability are not necessary to achieve such a powerful connection with who you are—the real you. What is required is an attitude of openness and willingness to be receptive to what unfolds. For me, personally, this route has provided enormous personal growth, satisfaction and joy, in addition to creating greater harmony with my self. It's all tied together, isn't it?

Realistic Self-Portrait. This exercise will help you to access your strengths and weaknesses more realistically. Consider your obvious physical, mental, educational, environmental and social realities. Avoid creating a fictitious picture, one in which you are all-powerful, knowing and thoroughly competent at all times. Let go of all those subjective, harsh, unrealistic criticisms, too. Remember that the average person underrates and shortchanges himself.

Once you have some data, go to a friend you trust and ask that person to help you select a series of words that best describes who you are. At first, this may be a source of laughter because few people, if any, ever ask this of those they trust. Be assured that you will receive important, accurate information as this friend begins to see how serious you are. Do this with anyone else who you feel could be objective and open to the idea. Next, go on an observation tour of your neighborhood and notice people who seem to have similar realities to yours. What you observe about them will often be true of yourself in terms of strengths and weaknesses.

Now you have a composite of information that should reflect who you are and what you can or can't do. From this list of descriptive words, choose those that you wish to incorporate into your daily definition of self. Imagine that these are individual ingredients (self-confident, patient, graceful, competent, caring, warm, generous) to be used in the following visualization exercise adapted for this program from the book *Superlearning* by Sheila Ostrander and Lynn Schroeder:

> While in a relaxed state with your eyes closed, imagine yourself sitting at a beautiful oak table upon which is a group of small mixing vessels and a drinking mug. The jars have labels upon which are written ingredients such as your self-confidence, patience, strength, gracefulness and excellence. Mix the ingredients you desire for yourself into the mug and drink it down. As you are drinking, feel all the ingredients you have put in the mug flowing through your entire body. Feel them being absorbed into your skin and organs and becoming you. When you have finished, visualize yourself standing up and going over to a wall that is one big mirror. As you look at yourself, see and feel yourself as the kind of person you are. Know that you will perform as you choose and be successful doing so. Say to yourself, "I will release all of the images that are preventing me from being all that I am; I will release any beliefs that will stand in the way of optimizing my full potential." Realize that afterward, the drink will still be taking effect within you, and all the things that you desire will continue to be a part of you.

Set aside a period of ten minutes each day in a quiet setting, go to your place of peace and repeat this exercise. Use as many of your five senses as possible in developing these images. "See" the liquid flow; "feel" the warmth and positive effect of the potion. The central nervous system will process these images as if they were real and erase any "old tape" by recording over it with one that is more realistic and accurate. You should consider this exercise as a means to develop any aspect of yourself that will bring you joy. Try it for twenty-one consecutive days and, coupled with the self-love exercises in Chapter Five, you will experience noticeable changes in attitude and behavior. Considering the number of years you put into the development of the unworkable images, this is not an extensive period of time. If it would be more helpful, try recording the exercise on a cassette tape and play it during your ten-minute alpha state.

Once you establish a realistic self-image, one that depicts the real you, you will begin to choose goals that are aligned with this self, and success will be achieved, which will increase your level of confidence. An augmented level of confidence, in turn, broadens the base for more success, which ultimately opens the door for potential realization and subsequent fulfillment.

People I Admire. Without giving it too much thought, list the five people you most admire (living or dead, known or unknown).

1. _____   4. _____
2. _____   5. _____
3. _____

Are you among those listed? Why not? Actually, very few of us would list ourselves. So include yourself now, if you haven't already, and proceed to write down next to each name the traits you most admire about that individual. What do you like about each person?

Are you like those people? Do you possess their traits? There's a chance you do. Even if their attributes seem unlike yours, consider that you possess these, on some level, but they remain latent. I contend that such attributes can be developed if you choose to do so. Using the mixing vessel approach, add these beliefs to the "ingredient" jars and visualize accordingly. Really "see" yourself behaving in such ways. In time, you will be what you "see." Imitate these people, when appropriate.

Think about actors who portray certain characters;

they actually become that "new" person. They talk about having difficulty switching back to themselves after having "played the role" for a period of time. Even animals can be positive models for creating change. While working with a world-class athlete, I discovered that his enchantment with a stallion enabled him to mimic the speed, power and grace of this black beauty. The athlete would visualize having those qualities and imagine himself gliding over hill and dale. It obviously paid off with a "number one" world ranking in road racing.

Activities You Do. You presently do or have done many things in your life on a regular, consistent basis, whether it be at home, on the job or at play. Oftentimes, these activities are a major source of your identity that contributes to the way in which you perceive your "self." Lackluster performance levels, for example, force you to think of yourself as inadequate; self-persecution results from these unrealistic, illogical thought patterns. Such self-distortion becomes the basis from which you measure your self-worth. In reality, you are not what you do or how you perform. The issue of "worth" is inappropriately attached to achievement and performance rather than what you are as a person. The value of what you do should be measured by your satisfaction, enjoyment, pleasure, learning and growing. Focusing on these will enhance your personal power and subsequent image.

The following exercise will help you discontinue self-abuse and harassment resulting from "worthless" performances. The key is to replace the automatic self-veto thinking with more meaningful, accurate responses.

On the chart below, list twenty things you do or have done on a consistent basis in your life. Include such things as housework, professional endeavors, athletic activities, relationship involvements, hobbies and creative outlets (music, dance, art, photography, writing). On a scale from 1 to 10 (low to high), rate each activity with respect to Enjoyment-Satisfaction and Proficiency-Performance levels.

After you have assigned a number for each one, go back and write the words LOW (for those numbered 1 to 4), MEDIUM (for those 5 and 6) and HIGH (for those 7 to 10). The way to interpret these results will follow at the end of this exercise.

Answer spontaneously. There are no right or wrong responses. This is simply an honest self-assessment.

ACTIVITY	ENJOYMENT-SATISFACTION LEVEL	PROFICIENCY-PERFORMANCE LEVEL
	ESL RATING	PPL RATING
1.		
2.		
3.		
4.		
5.		
6.		
7.		
8.		
9.		
10.		
11.		
12.		
13.		
14.		
15.		
16.		
17.		
18.		
19.		
20.		

INTERPRETATION. Any items with a rating of five or six can be disregarded for now; such a score indicates little or no effect upon your personal image. The major concern is with both extremes of the scale—the low and high ratings.

In the past (up until now), you would automatically measure your worth based on how well you do the activity (PPL). Close analysis should indicate a symbolic relationship between PPL and ESL. That is, notice how often your enjoyment and proficiency levels coincide. Most of us do well when we are enjoying ourselves, and vice versa. Therefore, if you've done poorly at something, could it be that you simply did not enjoy the activity? If so, lighten up on yourself; you didn't like the situation, and it has little to do with how good you are at doing it.

Conversely, the areas of your life where passion reigns will probably be accompanied by a high PPL. When your ESL is high, interest will soar and performance usually improves.

In either case, know that your performance is usually a direct outpouring of how much enjoyment and satisfaction you attribute to the activity, and has less to do with your level of competency. When you enjoy something, you put more effort and time into it, and the results usually materialize. With any low PPL rating, ask yourself this question: "If I had more passion for this, coupled with some good instruction, couldn't I do better?" The answer invariably would be affirmative.

There are some exceptions, however. For example, I love to play guitar but I'm not very proficient (high ESL, low PPL). The process is so much fun that my performance doesn't matter. Besides, I know that the PPL would rise with some good instruction.

Then there's the case of Low ESL and High PPL. For me, this usually occurs when I've been doing something for many years and no longer get any enjoyment from it. This is the classic "burnout" syndrome. Although you do a good job, it's not enough because it's not satisfying. When this happens, try to change the situation. After all, just being proficient at something is no reason for doing it. To continue will only create an obstruction to joy and fulfillment. Besides, why would you want to force yourself to do something you hate to do?

Affirm Who You Are. The use of positive self-affirmations (see Chapter Seven—Beyond Limited Affirmation) is another very powerful technique in helping you to create and maintain changes in self-image. This is nothing more than the suggestion (silent or voiced) of positive phrases to yourself. When repeated often enough, they become part of your belief system. This concept is not new. Many of your present beliefs about yourself are the result of years of negative suggestions from various people in your life. (Remember the awful teacher who called you a dumbbell?)

The field of advertising is a good example of how your thoughts and actions are influenced by suggestions. Millions are spent yearly to advertise products on television. Even political candidates have been elected on the basis of exposure on the tube, so there must be something to it.

You can take conscious control of those phrases you wish to have influence you. Choose scripts that are brief, positive and to the point, and that reflect the "real" you. Keep the phrase in the present tense and use rhythmic patterns, if possible. The exercise should be performed while in a deep state of relaxation (although not absolutely necessary), with each script repeated and visualized four times. Create personal phrases or memorize any of the following:

> Every day, in every way, I get better and better.
>
> I am in excellent health and great physical condition.
>
> My body and mind are one; I am in complete harmony and have lots of fun.
>
> I am confident, calm and centered.
>
> All of my negative self-images are now dissolved; I appreciate my talents.
>
> I am very special and unique. I like who I am.
>
> I like how I feel and enjoy how I think; I'm glad to be me.

As part of this exercise, imagine the world you create by using these words. These statements are truths about you, simple words that have the power to transform you into who you really are.

Veto Self-Vetoes. An important tool to use in helping to create a positive sense of self is saying "Thank you." Too often we reject compliments or words of praise with a subtle "put-down," a self-veto message. For example, someone says, "Nice job; you're terrific and do such good work." To which you reply, "It was nothing; anyone can do it." You discredit not only your efforts but also the person contributing the words of praise. A simple, "Thanks, I appreciate that" will reinforce your positive, real self. That's who you really are in that moment. You may have learned years ago that it is humble and polite to turn down compliments, but such false pride and humility will only serve to reinforce the negativism you have developed about yourself and will inhibit the process of getting to know who you are.

Uphold Expectations. Another way to help develop personal power is to avoid lowering the expectations that others have of you by telling them the negative aspects of your image. For example, the comments—"I haven't been in school for years", "I'm just going to see how it goes", "I've done no preparation for it" and "I could decide not to go"—may momentarily reduce the pressure, but such images will contribute to bringing about those spoken results (the self-fulfilling prophecy). Besides, you don't want others to think you're a liar, so you'll tend to live up to your "advertised image."

I suggest that "silence is golden." Let people have their expectations of you without your influence. I believe that if people expect me to perform well, I usually live up to those expectations. The self-fulfilling prophecy works for you in this case. Take their images of you and understand that they have good reason to feel confident in your abilities. They can always readjust those images based on your performance.

Shoulder Guardian. Your critical, elusive, internal monologue can be turned into a balanced dialogue. Talk back to that irrational critic by creating a gentle guardian on your right shoulder to answer, in a rational fashion, that critical voice on the left. When the critical self says, "You're no good; you don't do anything right," you can counter with the more upbeat and positive, "I'm just fine; I make mistakes like everyone else, but I profit by learning from them. I do many things right."

The nurturing self is the inner child, that unlimited being you have lost. When the abusive self pays a visit, say, "I remember you; you've been here a lot, but I was here long before you, so beat it!" Giving animation to these characters allows the mind to see the situation for what it is: a case of mis-identification.

Biographical Realities. So often, our self-image is sabotaged by a constant comparison to others who "really have it together." This is the old "appearance versus reality" trap; "Gandhi was so peaceful, happy and gentle, and I'm not." It seems as though he was a perfect spiritual model until you read some of the more insightful biographical sketches and learn that he, too, had to struggle to maintain a philosophy of non-violence in his personal life. In his own words, he said that "life is a constant vigil." By reading about his life, one quickly realizes that we all have similar personal issues; in the process, self-acceptance becomes easier to attain.

Read the biographies of those you admire and learn that we are all together in the universal struggle to grow and learn. Such reading helps to put the world in perspective and affords you the opportunity to not be so hard on yourself.

The key to the transformation of self is to *believe in the unique power within and use it.* There is no one else like you in the world—never has been nor will be. When you begin to be who you are, your world will start to blend and harmonize. When people become committed to doing what they are taught to do, they alter destructive patterns and become inspired and passionate beings. The key is to *assess who you are and act accordingly.* Work, however, is required; it's not easy, but the alternative is equally as difficult. There really are no other options.

Please trust that you are much more than you give yourself credit for. Don't underestimate yourself and limit your personal power. You will only go as far as your perception of who you are. Throughout the ancient Chinese book of wisdom, the *Tao Te Ching,* personal power is discussed as power over one's reality; it has the potential to bring joy, happiness, freedom and fulfillment into your life and the lives of all those who share your world.

CHAPTER SEVEN

BEYOND LIMITED AFFIRMATION: THE ULTIMATE LANGUAGE

The words you use create your reality. Keep them positive and they will provide the power to transform the quality of your existence.

(An old Irish axiom)

AFFIRMATIONS AND THE WAY OF NATURE

Think back to the law of nature as it relates to beliefs (Chapter Four): *Your world is directly affected by the strength of your beliefs; your beliefs become your reality.* Affirmations are the verbalized counterpart of these beliefs. They serve as reinforcers and strengthening devices for these "inner truths." So, in this sense, affirmations play a significant role in the direction your life takes; such verbal expressions will potentially limit or expand your performance or path in life.

Affirmations are a natural process; you use them daily whether you are conscious of them or not. And these "tapes" keep playing in your mind until the script becomes intentionally changed or rewritten.

Since the law of affirmations says that *your words. pave the way for the direction in which your life goes,* the purpose of this chapter will be to create an awareness of our self-limiting phrases, to consciously change the script and act accordingly. Be aware that this work will be facilitated by including the principles and tools discussed in the chapters on beliefs, self-love and personal power. In addition, visualization can be called upon, once again, to help go beyond the limits of language.

How can affirmations limit performance and misalign one with the way of nature? The following true story gives some insight into this question.

> Paula, a local "hotshot" runner, arrives at the site of the race one hour prior to the start. Noticing two "out-of-town" stars (both of whom she is faster than), she says to herself, "I guess 'first' is out of the question." Already her language indicates "failure." Her negative self-talk continues: "I feel tired today...I'm so stiff." Thoughts of defeat creep in, and she states that "I can't beat them today." *The word 'can't' is the most powerful limiting utterance in our vocabulary.* If you say, "I can't," you probably won't do anything to make it happen.
>
> As the race begins, Paula says to herself, "I don't deserve to win." Having this crucial belief verbalized thus reinforces its validity. "I'm not as good as they are," she says, even though she leads the race for the first three miles. "I shouldn't be in the lead." She thinks the other runners are holding back because they know something that she doesn't. Paula continues to sabotage her efforts, and her pre-race prophecy is fulfilled.

In effect, Paula was creating a distorted self-image based on fear. She proceeded to act out her new "role," which prevented her from realizing her full potential. This new image began to affect all aspects of her life for quite a while, at work, in school and at home. Everything seemed to be going wrong.

As you can see, her attitudes and beliefs about herself were molded by the words she chose, which, in turn, affected how she ultimately performed. Changing the words is crucial to the alteration of beliefs and behavior. What Paula needed to do was to align her statements and thoughts with her true potential, to blend the words with the abilities.

A classic example of such alignment is shown by the famous words: "I am the greatest, I am the greatest!" And who would have questioned the great Muhammad Ali, one of the greatest prize fighters who ever entered the ring. His words were a clear, honest, accurate, mirror-reflection of his talent. He knew who he was and affirmed it over and over again. Harmony between one's level of ability and the words chosen to describe it is an important consideration for both performance and fulfillment. What would happen if I chanted Ali's affirmation? I'd step into the ring and be carried away on a stretcher within seconds!

Very few people are "the greatest" anything, and I would suggest modulating one's enthusiasm about using such extreme affirmations. I have no qualms about saying, "I am one of the greatest dads," because it's realistic and opens the door for anyone to step inside if they so choose. In this way, I'm not excluding anyone, since there is room enough for all of us to be splendid fathers.

WHAT ARE AFFIRMATIONS?

Affirmations are very important components of the visualization process. They are strong, positive statements about something that is already true or has the realistic potential for being so. To affirm means "to make firm." So, affirmations are conscious, pre-planned, positive thoughts that help to *align your behavior with who you really are*. Without them, you leave this alignment to chance, and the possibility of desirable behavior occurring diminishes. Affirmations are also attempts to change patterns of negative thought that, like a broken record, continue to repeat themselves.

As with visualization, affirmations are tools applicable to practically all situations in life where self-talk creates disharmony with nature. For example, during those times when you are particularly self-critical, consciously choose affirmations that help to alter the negativity. Say out loud: "I am worthwhile and competent; I deserve the best there is; I have much to offer."

Perhaps you desire to change your physical appearance. Say to yourself, "Slim and trim, I am so thin." By so stating, you will create the proper mind-set, or environment, to accomplish this. You will become more willing to do what's necessary to achieve your image, and it will come to pass.

Affirmations can be used, too, if you wish to be more loving, self-accepting, friendly or appreciative, or if you wish to feel good, develop relationships, become more creative or confident, improve concentration, sharpen your skills or even cope with fatigue. The possibilities are only limited by your imagination.

GUIDELINES FOR THE CREATION OF AFFIRMATIONS

In order to formulate a workable, powerful, effective affirmation, certain guidelines must be adhered to. Incorrectly formed phrases can actually become negative statements in disguise. For example, "I will not get sick" might be interpreted by the mind as "I will get sick", as the brain generally does not process negative words. Once you learn the following principles, the construction of positive self-affirmations becomes an easy process.

Be positive. Affirm what you want, not what you don't want. This is the simplest way to avoid the negative. "I will not overeat today" may be picked up by the brain as "I will overeat." Instead, say, "I am eating lightly today."

Be present. To focus your statements on the future will be literally interpreted by the mind as if it were still coming. The future becomes a wish that stays right there, always coming but never arriving. Rather than "I will be happy," say, "I am happy," even if it's not true yet. Act "as if," and it will place you in position to activate the appropriate mechanisms to bring about the desired result.

Be concise. If affirmations become too wordy, you tend to become lost and confused with the verbiage, and so will your mind. Simplicity is the key to remembering them, as well. Being specific should help the process.

Be rhythmic. Although not crucial to their formulation, a cadence and rhyme in affirmations will tend to be more deeply impressed into your central nervous system. It helps with retention and can become a mantra for meditation. For example: "I'm in position to strike and get what I like," or, "Better every day in every way."

Be relaxed. The effect is more powerful if affirmations are said in an alpha state of relaxation (see Chapter Three). While relaxed, visualize what you say; don't just recite the words. Attach the statements to some vivid pictures in the "movies of your mind."

Be conscientious. It's better to repeat affirmations fifteen times, twice a day, than to wait for Sunday and devote one full hour. "Every day I say the way" is a good affirmation to help you be consistent. You might want to write each one on a separate index card and carry them in your pocket. Tape them to your bathroom mirror to recite before breakfast and before retiring.

Be optimistic. Expect success. Suspend disbelief and doubt for the time being. As when you turn on the faucet and expect water flow, so, too, expect change and positive results.

Be-gin! There's no time like the present. Begin to formulate at least one good affirmation for your list. Self-talk is a habit. If you repeat your phrases fifteen times each, twice a day for twenty-one days (that's how long most learning theorists say it takes to form a habit that becomes integrated), you will predictably begin to notice subtle, if not overt, changes in how you feel, act or behave. The process will bring much fun and joy, regardless of the degree of success achieved or the actual outcome.

TO ACT ACCORDINGLY

Naturally, you will want to create specific personal affirmations tailored to your particular issues, desires, needs and behaviors. There are many ways to create positive change in your self-talk, and these exercises will facilitate that process.

For the next exercise, however, you will be able to choose some useful generic possibilities to help you begin immediately. If the words "fit," say them...again, and again and again.

PICK AND CHOOSE, FEEL FREE TO USE

Ability
Calm and confident, I work well.
Effortlessly I glide like a tireless ride.
    (Good for aerobic sports)
Every day I flow with the way.

Self-Direction
Expect success; I am one of the best.
Failure is opportunity, dressed in disguise.
I act like a rudder, and steer straight to my goal.

Health
Healthier and stronger, longer and longer.
Health is me; I'm injury-free.
My limber, flexible self restores itself to health.

Confidence
I perform in good form, well above the norm.
I improve with each move; I'm in the groove.
I have confidence and trust in my abilities.

Self-Image
I love who I am, unique and with a

wonderful physique.
People enjoy me for who I am; they listen and glisten.
I am full of life; life is full of me.

Courage
Risks are the key to an exciting, wonderful life.
Mistakes are the dues we pay for taking risks for a better life.
Failure is a friend to help me learn.

PRACTICE TIME

Now that your generic choices are in operation, begin to notice some specific ways you create self-talk. Consider all areas of your life and include the above topics, plus financial concerns, sexual issues, success, relationships, work, play, love and forgiveness. Write down four of your favorite self-made verbal traps. Practice your skill of writing affirmations by changing each one to a positive counter-statement:

> **Negative Tape:** I always tighten up in pressure situations.
> **Changed To:** Loose as a goose, I flow with the show; or, Pressure is a time during which I perform best.

Negative tape: _____
Changed to: _____

Negative tape: _____
Changed to: _____

Negative tape: _____
Changed to: _____

Negative tape: _____
Changed to: _____

Since nature sees to it that you respond to your words, things will begin to change for you immediately. Say to yourself at this moment, "I am now willing to change in ways that make my life more fulfilling." It may require a few days to a week to become aware of your self-limiting language. Take all the time you need. The exercise is a process, not a product.

ASPIRATION AFFIRMATION

Affirmations are wonderful partners to the process of goal attainment (see chapter on direction). Assuming that you are experiencing fulfillment in the moment, you might want to think of ways to enhance and perpetuate this state in the future. You can plan to create environments at work or at home that will increase your potential for more joy.

In the left column, record three or more short-term goals, wants or desires that will enhance your fulfillment. Use the right side to change these goals into workable affirmations. The goals should be wide-ranging so that they include professional, spiritual, personal, familial or social aspirations.

Short-Term Goal	Aspiration Affirmation
1. To be less self-critical of my work.	1. "I am a diligent, competent person doing excellent work.
2. _____	2. _____
3. _____	3. _____
4. _____	4. _____

When reciting affirmations about a situation that hasn't yet evolved, you may experience difficulty imagining something that's not presently real. You may not believe it because it's not true...yet. With practice it will become easier. Remember that this isn't self-deception, it's self-direction based on strong likely possibilities. If you simply act "as if," you will set in motion various processes:

> It will raise your confidence level.
> It will reduce fear of failure and permit you to take a risk more easily.
> It will allow you to project positive images toward that goal.
> It will make it easier for you to do what's required to bring the desired goal to fruition.

QUANTUM QUALITY QUIZ

You and I have more positive qualities and attributes than we realize. However, we rarely notice or give ourselves credit for them. We have a difficult time saying good things about ourselves out of fear of appearing conceited. False humility traps us into believing we are less than what, in reality, we are.

Using the results from the previous exercises, talking to those you trust when defining self-image (Chapter six on personal power) or just noticing what you like about yourself, write five personal attributes or qualities for each of the following six areas as they pertain to your life (a total of thirty qualities). Give this some thought; you may have to do this over a period of days. Next, turn each attribute into a workable affirmation, using the previously discussed guidelines as much as possible. This exercise will enable you to stretch your mind and tune into your real self. It's an excellent way to formulate a concrete self-image, as well.

PHYSICAL _____

SPIRITUAL _____

PROFESSIONAL/OCCUPATIONAL _____

EMOTIONAL _____

SOCIAL _____

ATHLETIC (IF APPROPRIATE) _____

AFFIRMATION APPLICATION

Following the creation of a number of personal affirmations, choose half of those that represent your more crucial or im-mediate concerns, and place each one on an individual in-dex card. Those that remain can be placed in a folder for use in the near future. The affirmations on these cards can be carried around in your pocket or placed at your desk or night table, ready to be recited during convenient free moments.

These affirmation cards can be used in addition to visualization and imagery exercises. Although they are most effectively employed in a relaxed state, you can also recite them under your breath while walking around or, for exam-ple, waiting for a bus. Once you have memorized them, try affirming in the shower or while looking in the mirror as you comb your hair. While driving in your car is also an excellent time to recite your positive self-talk. Some people have even recorded their affirmations on tape so they can play them while driving or before going to sleep at night. Posting them in places where you will see them each day will give them even greater power and effectiveness.

Finally, try to incorporate them into your conversation by simply being positive toward others to bring out their best. When you give to others in this way, you are more likely to have them respond to you in similar fashion, returning the positive statements. In this case, there is no need for following the guidelines, other than remaining positive and direct. Be prepared to experience dramatic changes in your life; this works! *Affirmations will become beliefs.* Positive results will happen in ways that you can't even imagine.

A word of caution must be offered, however. If you are feeling particularly upset, depressed or negative, don't use affirmations merely to escape. If you do, it will simply repress those feelings, only to have them float to the surface at a later time. Instead, view these negative feelings as warning signs indicating that something is not right, and take action to ameliorate the problem. After so doing, introduce positive affirmations to build yourself back to a place of strength.

In order to reverse years of negative self-talk, you must become aware of how you criticize or limit yourself, whether it be on the job, at home or during play. From this awareness, challenge these statements and then substitute phrases that are more aligned with who you really are. NOTICE AND ACT ACCORDINGLY is an ideal affirmation to be kept on the tip of the tongue.

Finally, affirmations emulate the Tao as they attempt to bring the individual away from distortions and into close harmony with actual reality, the reality of who you are or what is possible given your true self. Affirmations are the language of possibility and change; their purpose is to remove the static, limiting impressions of the mind and create a transformation to a more unlimited, expansive and abundant existence. In his book, *Human Options*, Norman Cousins strongly suggests that the principal language of this age "must be concerned with the awakening of vast multitudes to the possibilities rather than the limitations of life."

When I was a little boy, I remember being frustrated when things seemed impossible to do. "I can't do it; I'm too small" were the phrases I used to get the help I thought I needed. My dad would often reply, "Now, son, you can do it; try, and if it doesn't work out, I'll help you." The outcome really didn't matter but the message, "Jerry, you CAN!" has been a guiding affirmation and attitude that has stayed with me for many years. It is, and always will be, the language of possibility.

CHAPTER EIGHT

BEYOND LIMITED DIRECTION: THE ULTIMATE JOURNEY

We must learn to differentiate clearly the fundamentally important, that which is really basic, from that which is dispensable, and to turn aside from everything else, from the multitude of things which clutter up the mind and divert it from the essential.

Albert Einstein

DIRECTION AND THE WAY OF NATURE

How would you feel if you valued peace and non-violence yet were employed by a corporation that made nuclear weapons? Or, what if you had a strong regard for health and life yet worked for the tobacco industry? Some people do, and they rationalize the obvious contradiction; others simply live in a state of constant dissonance and experience tremendous dissatisfaction, frustration, unhappiness and unfulfillment. Most of our lives are not such blatant contradictions, yet we still live our lives in the absence of harmony between what we value and what we do. We value health yet don't exercise; we value love and intimacy yet bounce around in relationships; we value peace yet choose to be right and fight; we value integrity yet compromise it each day; we value our family yet work so much that we can't enjoy them; we value freedom yet try to imprison our lives by not taking risks. Although subtle extensions of the more obvious paradoxes, these behaviors are still responsible for much of our unhappiness.

One of the laws of nature that influences how you feel in life indicates that fulfillment is measured by the distance that exists between what you value and what you do: the greater the gap, the more the dissatisfaction with life in general. The more the gap narrows, the more you experience a sense of well-being, joy and fulfillment. The idea is to create harmony between these two factors. Unlimited direction means to choose paths in life that follow your values, regardless of where the journey may lead you. I call this process INTEGRATIVE LIVING. It happens when you become aware of what you truly value and act accordingly. In other words, the direction you follow in life becomes aligned with your innermost values and concerns. Identify your values and set realistic, congruent goals in accordance with them.

It may initially appear that integrative living does not blend with certain aspects of the Taoist philosophy, particularly the concept of *wu wei*, "going with the flow." Setting goals seems to be a behavior that forces change upon our way of life, thus opposing or going against the flow. And, at times, it does. Many people, for example, try to "mold" their happiness by setting goals that bring only material gain, an ephemeral, shallow fulfillment at best. This is dangerous, according to the teachings of the *Tao Te Ching*, because such individuals are in harmony with dying, not

118

with change and growth. They become disconnected from the true meaning of life, the one that flows with internal fulfillment. John Heider, in his book *The Tao of Leadership*, reflects upon the materialistic path: "There is a problem with getting more and more. The more you have...the more you have to look after, the more you might lose...If you have inner security, you will have what you want anyway...you will be less harried." This is supported by R. L. Wing's *The Tao of Power*: "Being free of the desire for superfluous possessions...results in greater personal power." Your experiences in life will be much wider, paradoxically, with fewer attachments to uncontrollable material gain.

Unlike material quests, integrative living is an inner goal-setting process and can be viewed as a spiritual quest. Assuming you have fulfillment in the "here and now," you can go with that flow by aligning your goals with vital inner values and guiding yourself in this direction for future harmony and fulfillment. Your goals will be related to issues that reflect peace, joy, integrity, power, vision, harmony, love, health, excellence and achievement. Essentially, this affords you the opportunity to take responsibility for creating a life of spiritual, inner abundance. In this sense, integrative living is a process in harmony with "the way." Your world is an ever-changing, dynamic reality; this is "the way" of nature. To be in concert with this evolving force, you need to contemplate your world and dream things that never were. Through such vision (VISUALIZATION), you have the power to create breakthroughs ·in your personal spiritual world. Setting appropriate goals is an important aspect of this process. It is in harmony with the goal of the Tao: Align yourself with the changes and rhythms of the universe and direct your future accordingly. In this sense, we create that future by setting appropriate goals.

It should be stated that goals for material gain are not inappropriate within this framework. A nice car, house, stereo or other tangibles can be wonderful components to joy

and satisfaction in life. You deserve such comforts and lux-
uries and should include them in your universal plan. Be
aware, however, of the dangers involved in seeing these
material goals as the ultimate way to happiness. Such direction is usually devoid of the inner abundance so necessary
to the unlimited, fulfilling journey.

I'M BOOKED 'TILL I'M NINETY-ONE.

During a television interview a number of years ago, come-
dian George Burns was asked about his tireless energy and
long life. He responded: "I'm booked 'till I'm ninety-one; I
can't stop now." He exhibited purpose, hope and direction,
three important ingredients for a meaningful life. He claimed
to be constantly fulfilled because of this. Burns is also his
own person; he decides what's good for George and
disregards the opinions and expectations of others. After all,
that cigar may not be a tool for longevity, but it's fun.

There is an important lesson in this for all of us.
Before choosing your direction in life, consider what is important for you. Follow your passion. The key is to take the
path that brings the most joy and the least amount of
resistance. Following others' directives can create much havoc
and chaos. Remember that much of your fulfillment in the
future is determined by the course you take. Don't be led
astray by the opinion of others who may not have your best
interests in mind.

TO ACT ACCORDINGLY

The purpose of this section is to help you create a strong
awareness of what you value in life and then, through a
detailed process of self-direction, to help you set realistic
goals in accordance with those values. In a notebook or on a
separate sheet of paper, answer the following four questions.
If you keep a journal, you may wish to mark an entry there
for future reference. VALUES, remember, are those deep-
rooted aspects of how you personally view life and what's

important on an inner, more spiritual level. For example, you don't value running—you value health—while running is a mere manifestation of that value, something you like, enjoy or even love. You don't value your job—you value achievement, excellence and recognition—and your work is an extension of those values. Integrity, honor, justice, peace, harmony, intimacy, independence, dependability, freedom, security, honesty and trust are some of the more basic values that seem to be important to us.

Contained within each question is a series of other questions or statements that will help you to illuminate your values for the goal-setting process.

1. What are FIVE values that are important in your life?
To assist you in your awareness of values, consider, for example, how you spend your money, as one indicator. Also, what do you do with your time? How do these compare to what your life is presently like? Are they aligned with what you do?

2. What would you do if you were guaranteed success in whatever you attempted?
Why are you not doing it now, or at least some small part of or approximation to it? Your *choice* is a clear indication of something you passionately enjoy. To put it on hold or not include it in your goals is to be deprived of joy. Because time and money seem to limit our activities and dreams, the approximation of this choice is a viable alternative. Your choice is probably connected with some of those values in question one. How can you create movement toward this passion?

3. What are FOUR of your greatest personal achievements?
As you identify these, be aware that these achievements do represent areas of life that you enjoy. These accomplishments were quite fulfilling and are probably connected with your strongest values. That being so, what is your life like now because of these achievements? More than likely, you have benefitted tremendously. Therefore, what possibilities are you

considering for the future that will bring to you similar feelings of fulfillment? For me, my achievements are being a parent and writing a book. To recapture that joy, my wife and I are expecting a baby and I'm working on this manuscript. I value intimacy and achievement, and therefore I am creating the alignment.

4. Among the qualities your friends, colleagues and business associates possess, what FIVE would you enjoy having identified with your name?
The qualities you choose are probably those aligned with your values. What are you doing now, therefore, to assure yourself of such recognition? What plans do you have to place yourself in position to be so identified? By applying appropriate action, you will narrow the value-goal gap.

Notice your responses, and see if there's a consistency between your values in question one and what you'd like to do, now or in the future, or have done in the past. If there is a consistency, then you have some data from which to make some harmonious plans for integrative living. Your achievements, successes and positive recognitions are wonderful food for fulfillment. The idea is to plan to repeat such accomplishments in order to perpetuate these good feelings.
      You are now in position to begin a self-direction program. Be aware that goal setting is directly influenced by the following:

> Goal setting is accomplishing your specific purposes in life through a process of systematic growth.
> Personal growth will be accelerated by an openness of the heart and mind, a willingness to examine and transcend beliefs and attitudes.
> Judgment, criticism and defensive behaviors interfere with the growth process. You need to open your heart for change.
> Growth may not be possible in all areas of life. You

must consider your realistic limitations, accept them and change course.

You are your own worst enemy with respect to change. You have much more ability and potential than you can imagine.

SELF-DIRECTION WORKSHEET

With each of the following categories, write a short paragraph describing your ideal plan in relation to your values. Believe and act AS IF this scenario were possible, unless you have objective data to prove otherwise. Stretch and expand your imagination; let yourself go wild. Choose a script that creates passion and love for that particular item. This will increase your motivation and commitment to the plan. For example, I have enormous passion for my work. I have experienced few, if any, Thank-God-it's-Friday weeks. And my work evolved as a dream, just the kind of dream I'm asking you to consider for yourself. Don't think too hard; it's only a list, and it can be changed at will. Use a separate sheet of paper if you need more room.

1. WORK/CAREER: _____
_____
_____

2. PERSONAL GROWTH/SPIRITUAL: _____
_____
_____

3. EDUCATIONAL: _____
_____
_____

4. RELATIONSHIPS/EMOTIONAL: _____
_____
_____
_____

5. LEISURE/TRAVEL: _____
_____
_____

6. FINANCIAL/MATERIAL: _____
_____
_____

Now, once you have the scripts completed, follow these
guidelines to create specific short-term goals:

> List the overall, top ten most important goals from the
> total six scenarios. They could all be from one
> category or spread out in different ways.

> From these, record a list of goals to be achieved in
> five years. For example, "owning a home on five
> acres of land" would be appropriate.

> List five or six one-year goals that will put you in
> position for your "five-year" plan. Perhaps you'll
> begin by purchasing an inexpensive starter home
> this year.

> Record your six-month goals. For example, you can
> begin to actually look for property in six months.

> Record your one-month, one-week and one-day goals,
> all in conjunction with the preceding ones. The
> goal for this month would be to contact a realtor;
> your one-week goal would have you asking various
> friends for names of agents. Today, think of friends
> who could help.

This format can be used with any goal. It does not oblige
you to follow it. In a short period of time, it will become
automatic; you'll find yourself planning in concrete, detailed,
precise ways as if it were second nature.

CREATING ATTAINABLE GOALS

Believe it or not, goal realization is simply a process of
following certain criteria. Failure to do so can create disappointment, frustration and loss of motivation. The establish-
ment of objectives in a creative fashion is perhaps the most
important aspect to reaching your goals. We all set objectives,
yet those who achieve them seem to have a systematic way of
creating a plan that is easily attainable. The following five
categories will help you to set goals that can become your
reality:

1. Be Realistic: You must begin by being honest in evaluating
what is possible. First of all, the goals you choose should be

in concert with your values and lifestyle—not too ambitious, yet not selling yourself short. I remember when I decided to attend graduate school, seven years out of college, and wondered: Can I do it—is it realistic? Am I too old? Am I smart enough? To shed some accurate light on the situation, I engaged in a two-step process of investigation.

First, I talked to three close friends and confidants who knew me quite well. I announced my plan to go back to school and told them my deepest fears and concerns. Their responses were extremely encouraging, and I knew they weren't just trying to bolster my "fragile male ego." This gave the confidence to try step number two. I arranged opportunities to talk with others in attendance at various graduate schools as a way of seeing for myself if they were or were not more endowed intellectually. Although it was difficult for me to remain objective, I still received a clear picture of what it might take to "make it" in such programs. From what I could observe, I liked my chances for success. These were average people with no special qualities; they simply believed they could do it and were not hounded by irrational self-limits. They expressed insecurities similar to mine.

At this point, I felt I had enough "objective" data to support my decision. I followed through with confidence and the rest is history. I continue to use this approach on some level any time I wish to gain a sense of reality about the goals I wish to pursue.

2. Create Success: As you will see in the chapter on courage, simply taking the risk to create a life of harmony is the measure of success. This is a positive process that does not rely on outcomes for validation of its worth; a team can be successful even if the scoreboard indicates otherwise. Regardless of what may happen, you start the journey with instant success.

Now you will want to consider how to maximize the opportunity to realize your goals. Once you have established realistic objectives, create short-term goals that provide positive feedback. Your long-term objective may be to become an accomplished guitarist, for example. That could take years before success was obtained. Instead, try for an immediate payoff: This week I will find a teacher. When you do, consider it a success. Once you find instruction, your goal might be to purchase a good secondhand guitar. In this way, you begin to experience movement toward your long-range objective. Your confidence will rise as will your image of self. This will contribute to an increased level of motivation and commitment. Satisfaction and fulfillment are available now, rather than at some time in the future. In this way, *you take responsibility for creating and achieving success.* Since there is a tendency to continue with situations that bring success, you are storing "money" in the bank for that long path toward becoming a musician.

3. Establish a Challenge: If you set challenging, compelling goals, your motivation toward that destination will flourish. The key, of course, is to be sure the challenge is realistic. Surely, running the Sahara Desert would be a demanding task, but probably not wise to do. How do you determine whether a realistic goal is a challenge? Simply use your intuition (see chapter on intuition). Whether something is a challenge or not depends upon the individual. You know yourself better than anyone; you just have to trust your feelings. Your initial, gut reaction to the question, "Is this a challenge?" is usually an accurate indicator.

Once you choose the goal, you will quickly discover the level of difficulty. If you are in "over your head," readjust; if it's too easy, upgrade. The key is to find the balance between the two.

For additional input, consult with your boss, coach, spouse or other confidant as to what they think would be personally challenging to you. The final decision, of course, must be yours; however, the perceptions of others may reinforce what you already sensed. This is an additional vote of confidence that is so nice to have prior to taking on the task.

4. Be Specific: If you are interested in measuring progress, your objectives must be specifically stated. For example, you may wish to become more loving toward your child; what does this mean and how will you know when it happens? A realistic, short-term, specific goal may be: Today, I will hug and kiss my child and tell him how much I love him. This can be measured and the payoff is immediate.

How about at work? Your goal is to be more productive; but this is too vague, affording little or no direction. Try something like: This week, I will write six pages a day; or, call four new clients by Friday; or, make _____, bake _____, take _____ or rake by _____.

Charts are a motivational device that rely on specificity. Record your progress each day and experience the reward as you watch the graph line rise toward your destination and beyond.

Another helpful tool is the "DAILY DOZEN" sheet. For the past five years, I have recorded twelve daily goals on a pad each night before going to bed. I may want to run, shop, write, call certain people, see a number of clients, cook dinner, clean out my desk, read fifty pages of a good book, play with my son, have lunch with a friend, watch a favorite show and take the car in for a tune-up. When I awaken in the morning, I am ready to roll. I proceed to check off each item when completed and experience a strong sense of satisfaction from accomplishment. It's immediate gratification. To create the balance in my life, I make sure there are many days where the goal is simply to become a "couch potato"; this, too, is a realistic, short-term, challenging goal.

5. Be Patient and Persistent: Nature has its way: all things in their time, when they are ready. A Taoist would say that the attempt to rush matters goes nowhere. The way of nature is to put things into motion, do what can be done and wait. It may take time to obtain your objectives. This is the natural law of perseverance; any worthwhile accomplishment in life requires perseverance. It's the 95% perspiration, 5% inspiration phenomenon. Richard Bach had his best seller *Jonathan Livingston Seagull* rejected for publication eighty-two times. Thomas Edison had countless setbacks before he solved the lighting problem. The first manned spacecraft to the moon was supposedly off target ninety percent of the time. Patience and persistence are the bottom lines to goal achievement. If your objectives are realistic, they will be yours in time. I have been at the doorstep of my goal and turned around and gone home because I didn't want to wait another day. Perhaps it just wasn't important any longer, or my frustration and impatience got the best of me. The goal was there, but I decided against it. This is true of ninety-nine percent of the goals we set. If you follow the above guidelines and persevere, you will reach your destination.

To help develop tenacity, determination and persistence, use visualization, in a deep relaxed state, and act "as if" you've arrived. Again, this is not deception but direction. It will strengthen the expectancy of goal realization; commitment and motivation will increase. With practice, the visualization process will reinforce and fortify your belief in a positive outcome.

Remember that the goal-setting process is one of trial and error; it is time-consuming, often resembling the "dance of life": two steps forward, one step back. Being impatient also creates stress, which can cause additional interference with goal attainment.

Setbacks are to be expected; they are a natural consequence of taking risks and trying to create a fulfilling life. They are temporary, however, and represent opportunities to learn and reevaluate the situation. With your new-found data, you can establish new goals and proceed accordingly. More on this in the chapter on courage.

6. Pointers to Ponder: To complete the process of setting objectives for a more optimal life, remember the following:

Don't sell yourself short; you are more capable than you imagine.

Follow your dreams, not those of others, unless they coincide.

Progress is a roller coaster.

The goal may not be in your best interest; let it go if this is so.

Hold on lightly; something better may come your way.

USEFUL SUPPORT SYSTEMS

The road to your destination can often be a lonely one, with many obstacles. You may want to consider a number of support systems to help the flow go more smoothly. Use these, especially when you experience an emotional lull along the way. They may "help you through the night."

Incorporate Your Goals: Combining your goals with others' goals can be the source of much joy and fulfillment. For example, an amateur photographer who runs marathons is married to a woman who loves to travel. They both enjoy family outings. They might consider an early summer trip with the kids to a beautiful place with spectacular views for excellent picture taking. While there, dad could run a race with the support of the entire family.

Get a "Goal Buddy": Find someone with mutual objectives. Take a class, join an organization for personal, spiritual growth or exercise together. You could be an endless source of encouragement and inspiration for each other when discouragement sets in.

Create Fun: The path you take, although serious, need not be somber. The more enjoyable it is, the more relaxed and focused you'll become; fun is the key to success with any journey. I recall the words of Alan Watts: "You don't sing to get to the end of the song." Let the process be joy. Known as a "philosophical entertainer," Watts's major concern seemed to be enjoyment and fun, both for himself and for the audience.

Develop Affirmations: Make your goals firm with words that communicate positive direction and good feelings. This will imprint the clear message upon the central nervous system. The mind will accept the thoughts as if they were true. See the chapter on affirmations.

Announce Your Objectives: Assuming that the goals are realistic, you may want to "go public" by telling those you love about your intentions. If used wisely, this could strengthen your commitment and motivation, as well as give your supporters a chance to rally around and encourage your efforts.

Integrative living is a wonderfully dynamic process. The joy and gratification experienced from such a harmonious lifestyle touch your entire world. For example, when your planned destination becomes reality, you immediately want to help those around you to experience the same. When you care for yourself in this way, you can't help but want to care for others as well. You become excited and overjoyed with the world you've created and want to "share the wealth." When viewed in this way, unlimited self-direction is for the good of all, a spiritual path that creates an environment where values and desires are aligned. This is the ultimate journey.

How and when your goals are realized is ultimately dependent on the way of nature. Things generally happen when the time is right. Patience is required. Chogyam Trungpa, a Buddhist meditation master and scholar, wrote in his book *Shambhala: The Sacred Path of the Warrior* that

> you begin to see that there are seasons in your life in the same way as there are seasons in nature...times to cultivate and create...times of flourishing and abundance, when life feels in full bloom...times of fruition, when things come to an end...and times that are cold, cutting and empty...Those rhythms in life are natural events...how things are. If you realize that

each phase of life is a natural occurrence, then you need not be swayed...by the changes in circumstances that life brings.

In this sense you become the ruler of your world, the director, producer and architect of your destiny. Harmony with nature, blending what you want with what you value, is the key to unlimited direction.

CHAPTER NINE

BEYOND LIMITED COURAGE: THE ULTIMATE FREEDOM

Man cannot discover new oceans
Unless he has the courage to lose
sight of the shore.

André Gide

COURAGE AND THE WAY OF NATURE

I had always tended to be somewhat cautious and conservative in my approach to life. I never took risks or chances...always played it close to the chest. Then, when I was thirty-four, my safe world received a tremendous jolt: I had a close confrontation with death. I was told I had a malignancy and was given less than a year to live...then, a miracle happened. A mistake in the diagnosis was made—a *wonderful mistake giving me a new lease on life. I quickly learned how tenuous and "chancy" life is—a risky proposition at best. I now believe that the only way to live is to take lots of good risks...Why not?*

These touching, enlightened words of wisdom were emotionally expressed by a participant in a COURAGE workshop I conducted. More than a few heads in the group were rattled that day.

Why do so many of us insist upon waiting to live until we are struck by catastrophe? We act as if life is forever; mañana becomes our mantra. We are so fearful of any growth and change even though, intellectually, we know how wonderful and exciting it can be. Risk is anathema because the price of potential setback or failure is terribly uncomfortable and frightening. "Taking" chances becomes a behavior to be avoided at all costs. Instead, we choose the safe, comfortable, emotionally stable life—or so we think. In actuality, the choice is an illusion. To not take chances or risks can bring, paradoxically, a life of regret, stagnation, loss and emotional upheaval as we lament what "might have been" for many years to come. The real risk, therefore, is to *not* take the risk; this guarantees unhappiness.

With respect to the law of COURAGE, the way of nature teaches us a multi-faceted lesson: An expansive and richly fulfilling life is a product of your willingness to act courageously in the presence of fear and take educated risks in spite of the potential setbacks or failure you may incur. This isn't to say that all risks should be considered viable. *Terra firma* is a better choice than *terra incognita* in the absence of proper prior planning and assessment. The goal is to enhance and enjoy growth and change in life, not to play Russian roulette.

This law of nature has three major components that need to be individually addressed in order to create ultimate freedom for a fulfilling, joyful life. There's courage, which means to have fear like everyone else but to act in spite of it; then there's risk, a necessary component for a richly rewarding life; and finally, there is the courage to risk failure and success, inevitable occurrences with growth and change.

Before discussing these elements of the law of courage and how to help yourself create a more rewarding life through risk-taking, how does one become misaligned with this law? Very simply, it happens when you choose, out of fear, not to take the risk.

For example, you are in a group of rather politically conservative people who are espousing the merits of President Reagan's military budget. You resist voicing an unpopular opinion at the risk of losing their approval.

Your decision to not make a timely career switch out of fear of change could also represent one of the ways you fail to act with courage, particularly if the risk is minimal.

Then there are the risks of being involved in a new relationship. Many choose a life of reclusion rather than risk hurt, rejection or loss. By so doing, they also create a misalignment with nature's way with regard to love; harmony and joy are embellished through intimacy (see chapters on self-love and love). In the same vein, such risks involve the decision to have children and the gratification that could accompany such a choice.

To not go beyond limited courage is to create a world devoid of emotional-spiritual growth and harmony. To not take risks is to cause misalignment with one of nature's most powerful laws. Consider that the most damaging and painful risk could very well be not taking the risk for a more fulfilling life and, in old age, harboring tremendous remorse.

TO ACT ACCORDINGLY

The purpose of this section is to help you align with nature by developing courage to take educated, calculated risks to improve the inner and outer quality of your life, regardless of the outcome of such chances. To do this, let us examine the

elements of RISK, FEAR, FAILURE and SUCCESS on an individual basis to simplify the process for increased joy and
satisfaction.

RISK

If you ever want to gain insight into how life works, ask
those who have been on the planet for awhile. Recent studies
of people in their seventies and eighties indicate that those
who report fulfillment and "high well-being" have lived lives
that involved a great deal of personal risk. Clearly, most
reasonable people would agree that a life of risk contributed
to a life of experience, depth and quality. However, by definition, a life of risk also includes error and failure. Yet the attitude of these "chance-takers" toward a setback of any kind is
that mistakes are an inexpensive price to pay for a rich,
fulfilling existence. A full life, one where you push the
limits of your creative, emotional, spiritual and personal
potential will necessarily include thousands of mistakes. If
you see them as lessons, you create a wonderful learning environment and reduce the fear of such failure a hundredfold.
As you will see, mistakes are nature's way of teaching those
who can notice the correct path to their destination with
minimal force or effort.

Take the next five minutes to answer the following
questions. My hope is that your responses will prove to you
the truth of what you are reading, of what you already know
to be true: RISKS ARE ENJOYABLE AND WORTH IT.

What risk have you taken in your life that has worked
out positively?

What was your initial fear before taking the risk?

Did that fear materialize? Was it rational?

How did you feel after the risk was taken?

How did this action affect your life then? Now?

If you haven't taken any good risks lately, your responses may
now encourage you to do so. Maybe you already are a risk-

taker and these qualities simply reinforce your lifestyle. But what if you have no memorable experiences with risk-taking? There may be many reasons for this. The following words should encourage you to get your feet wet once again.

First of all, understand that to take repeated sojourns into *terra incognita* without proper planning and assessment is sheer sophistry, at best. Such destructive ventures are a setup for failure. The stakes are too high. For example, if you asked me to dive off a boat into 48° water at midnight and swim two miles to shore in the rough sea, I'd decline. However, if it meant saving my child from drowning, I would do it without hesitation. I'd take the risk because the stakes are too high to not do so. The goal must always be assessed. Will the risk enhance my life, make it more worthwhile? Or will such a decision put my life in jeopardy unnecessarily? It may do both, and then you must weigh the options. There will be times when emotions, your inner gut compulsion, will override all logic. You simply must act in spite of what it may do for the career, family or bank account. Hopefully, preparation for that risk will maximize the chances for a favorable outcome.

The bottom line for the types of risk I encourage is the answer to the question: "What is the worst that could happen if I took the chance?" If you can live with the outcome, "go for it." If not, perhaps it's a good time to put it on hold and consider the alternatives. To help shed light on this query, solicit the opinions of others you trust, and observe those who have ventured into these "unknown" waters.

Once the decision to take the risk is made, proper preparation is in order. Some risks require leaving something behind—a job, a home, friends and roots. You need to emotionally recognize this so the shock won't devastate you. Preparation for an ocean venture or wildlife excursion needs to be done far in advance. Obtaining the best instruction for sky-diving classes would be advisable. If you fail to plan, you plan to fail.

Finally, when all these steps are completed and the time to risk has come, don't hesitate to listen to that "inner voice," your intuition (see chapter on intuition). Children do it constantly. One day, my son Daniel agreed to join me on a trip to the store. "Let's go Dan," I said, to which he replied, "I don't want to go, Dad." Confused by his sudden reversal of mind, I asked, "Why not?" The response: "Because." No reason—just because. He made an intuitive decision to change his mind. I need to do that more often, too!

When taking life-enhancing, educated risks, remember that the outcome is irrelevant. If it turns out unfavorably, notice the lesson that is offered to you. You limit yourself by overlooking this gift of nature. *Success is already yours for having taken the risk; the bonus is what you will learn from the setback.*

Once the risk is completed, be sure to praise and congratulate yourself or anyone else involved. Rejoice, feel proud and celebrate your COURAGE. Focus on the positive process of taking risks for improved gratification. Then, if there is a setback, be sure to view the mistakes, errors or failures as the dues one pays to be vibrantly alive. Such tolerance and understanding encourage and reinforce the process, enabling you and others to try again. Any negative criticism at this point could extinguish the flames of courage.

FEAR

Whether you take the risk or not, fear will always be present. Having COURAGE simply means to take action in spite of the fear. That's why it's called courage. Understanding the fear, however, enables those with courage to put it into perspective. They view fear as a normal, healthy occurrence to a wonderful life. It's the way of nature, part of the plan. To attempt to avoid it is to avoid life, to become incarcerated in a self-imposed prison of physical, emotional, spiritual and social scarcity (or is it SCARE-CITY?).

In an attempt to encourage us through fear and out of self-captivity, philosopher Alan Watts states that "the other side of every fear is freedom." And I believe it is the ultimate freedom, because *once you transcend the fear, you realize anything is possible.* The fear was simply a tough exterior for something whose power was only in its ability to keep you fearful; beyond that, everything works out. Many octogenarians claim that they were afraid and worried about many things in life, and later wish they hadn't because those fears never materialized.

That's not to say that risking change cannot be a painful process. Yet this pain must be weighed with the pain of not taking the risk, which may entail a life of deep remorse or regret. The question to ask, according to Watts, is *not* "Does this change or growth hurt?" but rather "Will this pain help to improve the quality of my life?" Paradoxically, getting away from the fear of the pain of risk by not taking the risk is, in reality, the real pain because you'll always wonder "what if?" Remember that people never die from the fear of change, but some have died from the anxiety, tension, regret and lack of fulfillment created by not "going for it."

To help put fear of any kind into perspective, consider these thoughts:

1. As in the Taoist principle of *wu wei*, let go and go with the flow. Do not force the fear away. Quoting Alan Watts again: "Let yourself be afraid and then you will release the fear." You blend and resonate with the fear and, like the Japanese martial art, aikido, you actually "defeat" this opponent by blending with its own force. When fear is confronted in this way, the way of nature, you learn that it was really nothing. To fight the fear, is to cause the pain. What you resist will persist. Yield to the force of fear; experience it and know that it's a *normal reaction* to change and growth.

2. See fear as an opportunity. Taking risks for change and growth creates the chance to experience a depth and breadth

in life that is difficult to imagine. You will be closest to the door of fulfillment when the fear is most powerful; such fear is opportunity in disguise.

3. Fear is not something that goes away. It is part of life; it is nature's way of telling you that caution is advised. (Imagine if you had no fear of sky diving.) It's the fear that prompts you to assess the risks and properly prepare. In this sense, it becomes a friend to acknowledge and embrace; but first you must get beneath its tough exterior and realize it's not that bad. Remember the story of "Beauty and the Beast"? She was given the choice of moving in with this intimidating monster or witnessing the death of her father. Choosing the former to save her dad's life, she confronted her enormous fear only to discover the kind, gentle soul that resided within the threatening exterior of the beast. It's a powerful lesson for all of us as we prepare to go beyond our limiting fears.

FAILURE

What you now want to consider is the courage to risk...FAILURE, that miserable albatross hanging around the neck like the proverbial "scarlet letter." The word FAILURE often conjures up nasty memories of youth when you experienced subtle pressures from parents and others to always perform well. This easily happens to a young child, particularly when compared to an older, more "perfect" sibling. Also, an "only child" may feel the burden of "doing it all" so as not to disappoint mom and dad. Parents are often guilty of pressuring their children to excel out of a subconscious desire to live vicariously through their youngster's achievements. The Vince Lombardi Syndrome—"winning isn't everything; it's the only thing"—is exhibited by many coaches, teachers and parents. Such a mentality could be responsible for much of the fear of failure experienced by these children as they approach adulthood. The message is quite clear: Failure means you're worthless.

This brings us to the notion of beliefs and behavior. Since childhood, we have learned to believe certain myths about failure that make it intolerable. Such beliefs are nothing more than self-imposed limits that can be examined and changed.

First, many believe that failure can be avoided. Not so! The greatest of the great could not escape it, so why should you? I've worked with top-ranking olympic athletes and performers from all walks of life. They all experience failure on some level. Failure, like so much of what we resist in life, is simply nature's way of expanding and teaching us.

Secondly, many believe failure is worthless. In actuality, it is a necessary prerequisite to success. Failure teaches us much more than our successes when we are instructed by nature. We learn from our mistakes. So many of us feel that we can and should perform perfectly the first time we attempt a challenge. This is a totally irrational and mythological expectation, perpetuated unfairly by those who had significant input into our formative years. Mistakes are a crucial aspect to any process of growth and development. Studies indicate that highly successful, creative people have a higher than ordinary tolerance for errors, mistakes and failures. They are willing to learn from the setbacks and push through those temporary "schooling" experiences.

And finally, failure is believed to be devastating. Disappointing, yes! But the feeling one expects to get as a result of setback and failure is generally exaggerated. As we will see in the following section, people can actually find success to be terribly disappointing as well.

Now that some myths have been shattered, do you feel better about taking the risk to fail? If so, read on for more encouraging words.

Most of us tend to equate failure, mistakes, error and loss, particularly emotional loss, with the word CRISIS. In this sense, taking a risk and failing—whether it be with a career change, a new relationship or relocation—can create a personal crisis. The Chinese word for crisis, interestingly enough, means two things at the same time: danger and opportunity. Translated, it means "opportunity blowing on a dangerous wind." Applied to our notion of failure, setbacks become an opportunity to learn, once you look beyond the meaningless, temporary outcome. The following flow chart shows how this works.

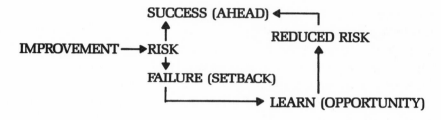

According to the laws of nature, it is impossible to fail. You need to accept the premise that all improvement in life— whether it be personal growth and development or change of any kind—requires a certain amount of RISK. Take the risk and you will either move ahead or experience setback. Traditionally, these outcomes have been confused with "success" and "failure," respectively. The new paradigm, the one in accordance with the laws of nature, says that your setbacks are opportunities to LEARN, to obtain more data, reduce the risk, try again and forge ahead, if not at first then certainly in the near future. Simply taking a calculated, reasonable risk ultimately is to be "successful." Real failure, therefore, is to not take the risk and always wonder what might have been. Even if you take the risk and never reach the destination, you'll always know you gave it a shot. Essayist Francis Bacon said many years ago, "There is no comparison between what is lost by not succeeding and what is lost by not trying." With the former, you can be assured of strengthening the foundation for consistent improvement and learning. Regret is what you're left with for not trying. Is there a choice?

I'm an avid competitive runner who recently experienced a setback in an important race. I fell short of my expected outcome goal by ninety seconds. At the start, there was a stiff tail wind. I could have taken advantage of that by going out faster, since less effort would have been required to run more quickly. Instead, I ran my usual opening pace quite comfortably, even effortlessly. At the turn-around, I headed back into the gale and was never able to make up those valuable minutes. I have since used this information to great advantage in an out-and-back, twenty-kilometer race. Each experience seems to be a wonderland of knowledge—*if* I choose to see it that way. The lesson here is to redirect failure and setback so that they work for, not against, you.

This principle of nature is easily illustrated by the martial art aikido, in which you blend with the direction of the opposing force, move with it and use its power to defuse the attack. This offers an interesting perspective on failure: See it as an opposing force, blend with it and use its lesson to your advantage for an inner resolution, much as the aikidoist resolves the conflict of the attacker. In either case, the power of the opposing force can no longer exist. You redirect the force and forge ahead.

In addition to this "new" view of failure, the courage for taking risks can be strengthened by the power of visualization (Chapter Three on vision). Understand that the fear of failure originates from images of impending doom; visualization can help to alter those negative, anxiety-producing pictures to images of hope and positive expectancy. As a result of diminished fear and tension, failure will be unlikely because *your level of performance increases when you're calm and relaxed.* Repeating images of success makes for a clear mental statement that increases your belief about positive results. In addition, visualization gives you the feeling of control, which also reduces fear. The psychological ramifications for using this tool are quite expansive; it places you in position to be emotionally receptive to taking risks and accepting the outcome, regardless of what it may be.

Risking failure may also be made more palatable if you consider minimizing the chances for setback and error. This may be accomplished by setting the stage for success through positive "self-direction" (Chapter Eight on direction). Choosing short-term, realistic, challenging goals will increase the chances of attainment, thus reducing the fear of failure. Integrated living, choosing a direction of personal passion, will fortify your courage to risk mistakes.

Finally, when courage seems scarce, and setback and failure become burdens, as they will on occasion, keep in mind the following thoughts:

> What will it matter in ten years? This helps you gain perspective on the importance of the situation at hand. In most instances, you'll realize it won't matter at all.
>
> Performance and taking risks are roller coasters.
>
> Nature's way says that "you win some, you lose some." It is irrational to think you can escape the ups and downs.
>
> Failures motivate. For all you know, your failure may be the impetus you need to push beyond self-imposed limits and barriers for a more expansive life.
>
> All well-known achievers and risk-takers have expansive, fulfilling lives because of one commonality: They possess a very high tolerance for error, setback and failure. They "bounce back."

SUCCESS

What about the courage to risk...SUCCESS? You would think that every one of us would welcome the praise, adulation and accolades that accompany success. Yet many of us shun the limelight; "making it" becomes a disguised form of the fear of failure, because once you are on top, there's nowhere to go but down. It takes courage to risk success, as it brings with it the pressures to maintain that position or risk "falling out of favor" and becoming a failure.

"Success has ruined many a man," wrote Ben Franklin; and, may I add, many a woman as well. I personally have seen the lives of olympic gold medal winners and politicians elected to responsible positions fall apart after their accomplishments because of the pressures to live up to great expectations. These people also had the tendency to become more lax with their talents, as they had achieved their primary goal and had nothing left to look forward to. They even talked about the disappointment they experienced when it became obvious that success was not "all it's cracked up to be." It rarely delivers on its promise.

The FEAR OF SUCCESS is no hocus-pocus, psycho mumbo-jumbo phenomenon created by psychologists to pad their wallets. The concept was first introduced years ago by Dr. Sigmund Freud, who noticed that people have a pattern of becoming "ill" just when they're about to attain success or just after a goal is realized. Ill in this case could actually mean to engage in self-defeating activities as well as, literally, "sick." Freud, in his articulate essay "Those Wrecked by Success," wrote that some people have difficulty enduring the bliss of fulfillment. This thought has serious implications for the journey we've been discussing. I have noticed that so many of us create unfulfilling lives because we fear the work required to maintain such bliss. Some of us feel we don't deserve such a life and have difficulty accepting it. It's crucial to notice if this is true for you; if it is, you will continue to sabotage all of your sincere efforts to change. Become aware of its subtle penetration; you may have the fear of success and, if you do, you may well lack the courage to risk attaining success. There are other related fears to be aware of, too:

Fear of Self-Knowledge: Most of us, at one time or another, resist knowing our potential. If you were to KNOW that you were quite good at something, you would feel compelled to act or else feel guilty about not developing that potential. And maybe you would rather not act; after all, developing this aspect of yourself may require hard work, trying to live up (in your mind and others') to that standard. Becoming totally committed to excellence in any aspect of life could mean time away from your job, your family or your friends. It's a decision that could have painful repercussions. As a result, you may choose a road that avoids success with all its pressures. Success, in your mind, becomes a frightening entity. However, if you turn your back on the possibility of success, there is another pain to contend with; you must grow old constantly wondering how wonderful life might have been. The regrets to come, as a result of *not* taking chances in the formative years, could prove to be an even greater burden than the difficulties you might have had as a "success." The choice is yours, and either is viable. Choose what's best for you. Being cognizant of this may make it easier for you to determine, and put into better perspective, what is more important. If you think you'll have regrets, "go for it" while you are still capable. If not, there's no reason to get down on yourself for calling a halt before success. Being good at something is certainly not the only reason for doing it. The bottom line is happiness through balance (see chapter on balance).

Fear of Unacceptance: The need to be accepted by all of your friends and acquaintances could develop within you a fear of success. Subtle pressure exerted by your peers and associates could force you to maintain the conventional, status quo lifestyle. Emotional, spiritual, professional or social growth and change could cause tension and force others close to you to become threatened. Adopting a vegetarian, whole health lifestyle may be wrongly interpreted as a rejection of their meat-eating, sedentary existence. Your own changes may force them to look inside, which may be uncomfortable for them. As a result, they could joke about or ridicule your growth, which will create feelings of alienation. Many of us would rather forego successful change than risk such blatant unacceptance. During the early 1970s, Dr. Matina Horner's studies showed how women were conditioned NOT to succeed. Extra pressure and tension were experienced by women who tried to break away from the traditional, stereotypical roles. Things are not that much different today because, although some of society's attitudes have changed over the last eighteen years, women still struggle internally with the double bind. They feel guilty for achieving beyond their female friends and feel like failures if they don't. It has become a double-edged sword.

The bottom line is to understand that if you grow, change and are successful, some people will feel threatened and be unaccepting. For you to feel twinges of anxiety and discomfort is quite normal; however, if you let it stand in the way of creating joy and fulfillment for yourself, you've got a problem. It could be of help to you to communicate your feelings directly with those who feel the resentment. Such a dialogue could begin in this way: "I sense some changes in our relationship; I feel unaccepted and ignored. My decision to change my lifestyle doesn't change my good feelings for you." Continue your journey toward happiness; those who truly love and respect you will stand by your side. What better way to test the quality of your relationships?

Fear of Disaster: Very often we will shy away from success because we erroneously associate it with the law of averages: Success must be followed by setbacks or disaster. Anything too positive must be countered with danger. How many times have you heard someone say, "Things are going too well. This is when something goes wrong...I better watch it"? And things do go wrong, not because they had to but because the images of setback created tension and anxiety, which contributed to the turnaround. People become convinced that if life is too fulfilling, it must certainly end. They can't believe life can be so wonderful, so they proceed to sabotage their initial efforts toward positive change. You now know better. You know you *do* deserve the best; we all do...always.

Perhaps the root of most problems experienced with success relates to your attachment to that outcome. Remember that you are successful regardless of the results, *because you took the risk.* Letting go of "success" outcomes is as crucial as letting go of the "failure" results. Both are lessons; both can be joy. If you insist upon identifying with these "successes" as if they were "you," then they will have the control. The Tao would indicate that when success is achieved, withdraw. Go on to other paths and forge ahead. In his book, *The Tao of Power,* R. L. Wing states that "after achieving success, do not linger to experience the inevitable cycle of decline." If you stop to dwell upon successes, "inner growth will end...All things that reach their full maturity... must necessarily decline," claims Wing. When your work toward the goal is complete, maintain fulfillment by moving on to the next destination.

Hopefully, you do not feel compelled to jump into a life of total risk-taking. The Tao would recommend that you do what comes naturally: If you are inclined toward taking a chance, consider the alternatives and act. Personal courage may be fortified by contemplating the thoughts within this chapter. In time, you will discover the wonderful inner rewards available with the expression of unlimited courage. Failure to risk the unknown may subject you to a self-imposed emotional prison; going beyond the fear and taking a chance creates the possibility of experiencing a sense of inner FREEDOM that could never be imagined.

CHAPTER TEN

BEYOND LIMITED INTUITION: THE ULTIMATE GUIDE

*There is more to the mind than reason
alone...there is something we frequently
experience—perhaps we can call it intuitive
awareness—that links us most intimately to
the universe and, in allegiance with the
heart, binds us together in generosity and compassion.*

Ram Dass and Paul Gorman
How Can I Help?

 INTUITION AND THE WAY OF NATURE

ne of the most important lessons we learn from the child is the importance of the intuitive mind; however, we rarely notice it. Every day some parent becomes angry, intolerant or simply annoyed at the absence of logic in the child's responses to rational questions: "Daniel, why don't you want to eat your dinner? You said you were hungry." To which the three-year-old replies, "BECAUSE!" Case closed!

That's it; no reason for further dialogue. And why should there be any explanation? "Just because" is the child's way of expressing what adults have lost touch with—the intuitive mind. If the child had the verbal capacity to match his emotional sophistication, he might respond in a different way: "Dad, I have a strong inner sense that food at this time would not be appropriate. I'm listening to my body and it tells me to change my mind and not eat."

Why, therefore, don't adults express themselves in this way as they have acquired the language? *Because!* Because even though their verbal abilities expand, the emotional component gradually contracts. The intuitive self becomes underdeveloped as we are taught from childhood to distrust our feelings. For example, a parent might say to a child, "Because...Because is no reason...It doesn't make sense." The demand for a logical, rational response creates a subtle message that feelings are not justifiable reasons for behavior.

Another way parents extinguish intuitive thinking is to discount the importance of a child's dream. "Daddy, Daddy, there's a monster in my bed!" The father proceeds to rescue the boy and say, "There are no such things as monsters," rather than explore what the child was intuitively feeling. The message, once again, is that feelings don't count; they're not important. "Let's look at it more logically" becomes the more "adult," mature approach. No wonder we all grow up suppressing our spontaneous impulses; we hesitate to question authority when the intuitive self sees other options. We seek the approval of others (particularly of our parents) while questioning our powerful intuitive sense. As adults, we idolize the logical, the reasonable. The rational becomes superior to the intuitive as we begin to suppress our feelings and avoid the emotions.

As a result, we learn to become extremely limited; we generally use a mere ten to fifteen percent of our brain's capability. Vast amounts of knowledge, answers to questions and solutions to problems are ours for the asking. I find, personally, that when I listen to my intuition, I have a ninety percent success rate. When I rely solely on my analytical, rational mind, that percentage drops considerably. The key to success, I believe, is to use a "total-mind" approach where the intuitive and rational become partners in a more complete, holistic view of your reality. The brain, naturally, collects information simultaneously from all stimuli, using both hemispheres—the right, intuitive and the left, analytical. We need to stop discarding the pertinent input of the intuitive side. This brings us (logically?) to the next law of nature, the way things are.

In the *Tao Te Ching*, Lao Tzu writes about intuition being the purest form of information. He impresses upon us the need to use intuition with logic as partners in order to view our world as it really is. Therefore, one of the most important laws of nature indicates that if you wish to learn about and blend with the world around you, begin to use and trust your intuition. The ultimate in fulfillment, according to the Tao, is to keep a constant vigil of nature, using the intuitive mind, and act accordingly. In order to experience joy, a holistic, total-mind view of the world is necessary. To rely on just one hemisphere, right or left, is to forfeit the balance and not function as nature intends. In his *Tao of Power*, R. L. Wing comments that by "continually augmenting one's external view of the world with information from the intuitive mind, one develops a sense of the continuous processes and patterns in life." By doing that, we increase the likelihood of creating a life free of misfortune and filled with happiness.

One of the more interesting aspects of this principle of nature is the way it facilitates the understanding of all the laws of the universe, particularly those talked about in this book. Surely you have noticed your initial reactions upon reading each law; you intuitively were aware of them and probably whispered, "That makes sense; I know that." Yet, have you kept an ongoing vigil or awareness and acted ac-

cordingly? Like most of us, you probably need to be reminded and have it stated as such before acting more in harmony with "the way."

This law of intuition, more than any other, requires
an inner harmony and balance, a true blending of the YIN
and YANG, the feminine and masculine, the intuitive with
the logical, in order to create an outer harmony with the
world as it is. In order to accomplish this, we need to gain a
greater respect for the power and usefulness of the
underdeveloped intuitive self. It is equally as important to
the creative harmony in life as the cherished left brain, the
logical, rational part of the mind.

Webster's New World Dictionary helps us to begin by
defining intuition as "direct knowing without the conscious
use of reasoning; immediate understanding and the ability to
perceive and know." The capabilities of our intuition are in-
finite and represent a huge reservoir of accumulated
knowledge. The most famous artists, scientists, inventors,
musicians and other luminaries could not have performed
without access to the right brain. Albert Einstein, for one,
has claimed that "my understanding of the fundamental laws
of the universe did not come out of my rational mind." You
are endowed with an incredible resource that has the power
to transform your life. With the ability to make better
choices, clearer decisions and to enhance your problem-
solving capabilities, your chances for joy and gratification in
this life are greatly increased. In conjunction with Chapter
Nine, perhaps you will have the courage to risk listening to
that inner voice, to trust that *you have within you all that is
needed to create the joy you deserve.*

"I know I should have gone" or "I knew it should have
been done that way" are the often-echoed expressions of
disappointment that accompany a misalignment with this
law of nature. Intuition is like having a good coach on a
basketball team: The leader brings the team together, causing
a harmonious blending for total fulfillment. Without such

guidance, the apparent talent bows to chaos and disruption. In life, our intuition guides our intellect so that we can blend with life in the best way possible—the way of nature.

An example of such misalignment happened to me years ago as I was embarking upon a new career. I was offered a position to teach at a college and accepted, in spite of strong feelings to the contrary. I intuitively knew "I should have declined" yet ignored this wisdom. Two weeks later, an incredible opening came at an ideal location for a wonderful job. It was too late and, worst of all, my inner voice had been right. My new job was totally intolerable. I have been giving a high priority to the input of my right brain ever since, and I'm a good deal happier because of it. My intuition has been instrumental in getting books and articles published, in developing career possibilities, and in following through with certain relationships, travel arrangements and decisions about leisure-time activities. The older I get and the more wisdom I accumulate, the more I follow my intuition to contribute to a joyful process of life. One of the teachings from the *Tao Te Ching* that seems to help me in this regard is the lesson of *wu wei*, going with the flow. The flow, in this sense, relates to the feelings of the intuitive self. When that inner voice tells me that "this isn't the best time or way" or "he's a good person," I become sensitive to this "sixth sense" and listen. That, to me, is natural—what feels good.

I recently read a story about a woman who decided to change her plane flight while at the airport. She had experienced strong intuitive feelings to do so. The plane she was to be on crashed upon takeoff, killing all the people aboard. Coincidence? Maybe, but she's alive today to tell about it.

This isn't to suggest that you change or create plans based totally on your feelings; there may be other logical variables to consider, other realities to cope with, and your decision should be based on all the data available to you. Remember that taking a risk means determining the possible consequences and then making a choice.

To start out, I recommend "playing" with your intuition. For example, the next time you intuitively feel it's better to not attend the party of a friend, stay home, even though there's a chance for social repercussions. Others may not understand, or think you're crazy. The payoffs, however, will be so rewarding that you won't worry about what they think; they may even begin to follow your path.

I do suggest that you begin with small, non-threatening, comfortable decisions and choices and, as you gain confidence, go forward from there.

TO ACT ACCORDINGLY

Before plunging into the sea of intuition, remember that errors, setbacks, mistakes and failure are inevitable. Such outcomes are one aspect of "the way" of nature, helping you to learn, regroup and advance. Keep in mind that reliance on the logical self alone will also subject you to setbacks and, perhaps, even more frequently. What you analyze, what you determine by logic and left-brained thinking, may not materialize with any greater success. Working with the concept of courage in Chapter Nine should facilitate the risk you need to take with this inner voice. And, remember to be kind to yourself; no self-criticism is needed when things fail to work out. An attitude of openness and trust, with yourself, will keep you from being judgmental. Patience with the process will ensure success.

It may be difficult, at first, to distinguish between the voice of intuition and the voice of fears, doubts, old beliefs and the opinions of others. There is no sure way to guarantee that what you are feeling is from the inner self. The following exercises, however, will increase the probability that you are clearly hearing your intuition.

SPIRITUAL GUIDE

Your inner self is always trying to communicate with you, yet the everyday stresses, anxiety, tension, fatigue and "normal" mind-chatter interfere with its attempt. Therefore, using the tool of visualization, you can create an alpha state, get to your place of peace and, from this tranquil location, silence the blocking forces and allow the intuitive self to make contact.

One of the most effective ways to do this is to create a "spiritual teacher" who will help to give you input into questions or problems to be addressed or decisions to be made. This teacher could be totally fictitious, a figment of your imagination, or a real person, a friend or perhaps someone famous that you may not know personally but you admire. Your choice could be anyone, from the beginning of time to the present. See this teacher as a very wise person, with much integrity, insight, clarity, humor and kindness. Give your teacher a name and invite him or her to your place of peace for consultation.

This may seem rather strange to you at first. However, all you are doing is giving your intuition a tangible identity. This teacher is your true inner voice, a reflection of what's happening inside of you, a mirror reflecting what you feel at the moment. In establishing this contact, you create a powerful source.

My adviser is J. Cheng, a very old Taoist, who doubles as a nurturing father as well. He lives very simply and is available to me at a moment's notice. We "meet" at my place of peace and discuss issues of concern. He has wonderful advice (INTUITIVE DATA) with regard to decisions, problems or questions. Sometimes we "play" together like two kids. His laughter is contagious.

Once you have chosen your teacher, begin to make contact on a regular basis. Invite this sage to your place of peace, and in a deep, relaxed alpha state, enjoy the ensuing dialogue.

To structure the dialogue, think of a question you have, a problem to be solved or a decision to be made. Present one or all of them to your adviser and say:

What do I need to do?

What do I need to know?

What do you think is the answer?

The most immediate response is normally a good indication of the direction to take. Trust the feeling; trust what you "hear" and act on it. If your teacher does not respond, more time may be needed; thank your teacher and plan to meet again soon. Perhaps your intuition isn't clear at that moment, or you are simply not ready to move on the issue at hand. Either way, it's your inner self talking to you, and your intuition knows what you need and when.

This is a powerful tool to be used often, particularly when you feel alone and need support. Although we can be our own worst enemy, we can also be our own best friend.

The trend these days in the corporate world is "intuitive management." Many scientists, inventors and executives are beginning to use the technique of the "inner guide" to tap their enormous amounts of accumulated knowledge. Our intuition is being accepted now as a universal library of accessible, accurate data.

THE QUICK FIX

So often we struggle over minor daily issues related to the process of life. For example:

Should I take this course or that one?
Should I cook tonight or go out to eat?
Should I work at home or go to the office?
Should I go to the beach or watch the game?
Should I invite some people or go alone?
Should I clean the house now or do it later?

Notice the questions. You're not trying to decide to have a baby, get married, move to another country, change careers or buy a house. But the kind of examples above do, however, force us to stop and think, and they often create frustration and unnecessary delay. This could be the result of trying to force an answer. The more you "press," the more tension you experience and, consequently, the more difficult it is to have clarity of mind. This is in opposition to the Tao, the concept of *wu wei*, which says that we must let go, go with the flow, in order to achieve. The idea is to give up the urgent need to search for the solution; it's already there. You simply must relax and trust that this is so. When you give up trying to find the right answer, it suddenly appears. You can facilitate this process by releasing the emotional, subjective attachment to the question and becoming more objectively involved. For each of the above or similar choices, ask these questions:

> What if I didn't have to make the decision *now?*
> What would the right choice be anyway?
> What if I knew the answer?
> What would it be?

The responses to these queries often come quickly and represent your inner, "gut-level" reactions. With some practice and trust in the answers, this tool will help you to cut through much wasteful deliberation.

DREAM OBSERVATION

Dreams are an extension of your intuition. They are a vehicle for discovering your innermost thoughts.

In the mountain region of Malaysia, there is an unusual primitive culture called the Senoi; they spend a good part of each day discussing their dreams for the purpose of personal growth and change. They are a peaceful, nonviolent group that thrives on sharing and cooperation. Psychological problems, as we know them, are nonexistent among the Senoi, and many believe this can be attributed to their intensive use of dreams to resolve problems and to create a life of peace, harmony and fulfillment.

You, too, can use dreams to contact the innermost thoughts of your mind. This natural, creative, alpha state is comparable to visualization and working with your spiritual guide or teacher. You can *consciously program* a dream to reflect upon what's happening in your life. I am not talking about deep, psychological, Freudian dream analysis, with symbolic imagery interpretation. Simply record your dreams and notice what they have to offer.

To program your own nocturnal scenario, go to your alpha state prior to falling asleep, using deep abdominal breathing. When relaxed, say to yourself:

"I am going to remember my dreams." Repeat three times.

Then say, "Tonight I will have a dream that will shed light upon..." (fill in the blank with your concern).

Before you go to sleep, visualize remembering the dream and recording it.

Be sure to have a pad and pencil next to your bed. The instant you awake, jot down all the details of the dream that you can remember. Write in the dark if you must; it will be readable. "Overnight" results are rare, but in a number of weeks you should have it mastered. If you would rather not use this technique, try recording dreams as they naturally occur (without "programming" them beforehand) and see if they speak to your concerns. Just be sure to keep your "dream notebook" close at hand because dreams tend to become elusive once you're fully awake.

PLAY IT BY EAR

When asked the question, "What do you want to do on Saturday?" I often respond with, "Let's play it by ear." Sometimes I enjoy *not* planning and wish to rely on my intuition to determine the appropriate choice when the time comes. I have had much practice with this over the years, to the chagrin of my friends who enjoy designing the future. I have paid a price occasionally for not plotting a course of action, but "playing it by ear" has always been more exciting, interesting and noticeably more rewarding. It is the ultimate lesson in *wu wei*, going with the flow. It optimizes options and allows you to respond in the moment, as you feel. At first, the lack of a plan may create some anxiety, but with practice, you'll actually relieve the stress that comes from searching for "the right" thing to do. Your intuition, if you trust it, will give you this information when it's needed.

Which of the following are you willing to begin with? Create some examples of your own.

> You're going on a day hike with some friends. Just choose the location and leave the rest to chance.
>
> Friends are visiting from out of town this weekend. Wait to see what they wish to do.
>
> Go to the supermarket and let your intuition determine a meal that you'll cook.
>
> You are going out for the evening with a friend. Decide where to go as you get ready to leave together
>
> You have a free day coming up; wait until it arrives and go with what feels best.

Naturally, the rest of the world's schedule may dictate the degree to which you can be that flexible. For example, holidays preclude shopping if the stores are closed, and you can't "play it by ear" if your choices depend on others being available.

STAY TO THE LEFT OF YOUR "BUT"

So many of your intuitive desires are nullified by rational thought or judgment, as if logic ruled. For example, notice how often the inner voice comes first, followed by "but" and the reason why it's best to not follow your "whims."

A worthwhile exercise is to notice when you make these statements and then stay to the left of the "but." In other words, do what you initially say and forget what follows the "but." The following are examples.

> I could really use a vacation *but* that's irresponsible.
>
> I'd love to go to the party *but* I need to get up early tomorrow.

I want to leave this meeting *but* I might be criticized.

I need to rest *but* there's too much to do.

I'd really like to get in shape *but* there's no time.

I really want to take that class *but* I might get too tired.

I'm really hungry *but* I shouldn't eat yet.

I really want to sing *but* I'll look like a fool.

I'd love to ask her to dinner *but* she'd probably refuse.

I want to quit this program *but* people will get down on me.

What are some of your ways of avoiding the "now"?

YOUR BEST GUESS

Practice using your intuition by listening to your best guess on the following items. What does your intuition say about...?

> tomorrow's weather
>
> the fastest route home (as opposed to the longer, more conventional way)
>
> the best entree for dinner
>
> the best color when buying an article of clothing for a present
>
> the next person you meet
>
> the best direction for a walk
>
> the best music album to buy
>
> the color of the next car to pass you on the street
>
> who it is that is calling on the phone
>
> which class to attend

AN HOUR A DAY IN ORDER TO PLAY

To further develop the habit of using your intuition, have fun by designating one hour each day to completely follow your inner voice as if it were totally correct. You may want to begin with an hour at home; work may be too threatening an environment, unless it's during the lunch hour. Do this for

seven consecutive days and notice your increased energy
level, how you feel more alive and connected with the world
around you. Once the hour has expired, return to your normal patterns. Begin to see how more of your time becomes
devoted to using the total mind. This exercise is very
enjoyable—it makes the day exciting.

It is only within the last three years that I have come
to understand my lifelong addiction to sports and sport-like
activities: SPORTS ARE BASED ON INTUITION, and intuitive living is joy—it feels so good! Understand that to intuit is to know by instinct, impulse, feeling, insight, sixth
sense or automatic response. Such typical characteristics are
essential to fast-paced activities and require a perfect blending with nature, a harmony of body, mind and spirit. To be
good at basketball, for example, one must constantly be
ready to respond instantaneously. Your sixth sense tells you
where to be for the pass that hasn't arrived yet. You instinctively know how to "shake" a defender and clear a path
to the hoop. Split-second reactions are rewarding; they feel
terrific—they are *intuitive*.

My inner voice continues to develop by my participation in "adventure running." I am ecstatic as I gallop through
redwood forests on ancient trails, or frolic in the Sierra
Mountains on terrain that demands instant responses or you
pay the price of injury. My mind is five steps ahead of my
feet, ready for me to react automatically to hostile boulders
and roots, even an occasional rattler. No time to analyze with
the rational mind. There's such joy to giving yourself over to
nature and "feeling" her patterns. While in the wilderness,
your confrontation with its natural inhabitants is a common
occurrence. I can't tell you how natural and instinctive it is
to run with the deer. They sense your playful posture and offer you challenges impossible to meet; however, blending
with their games is an incredible experience. Why?...
Because! (good response?) It gives you the chance, like a
child, to aimlessly play and follow your intuition. You

become one with the universe. All problems cease to exist. No decisions need to be made; you just go with the flow. The deer are wonderful teachers, offering valuable lessons in harmony as they so beautifully blend with nature's gifts.

Most recently, I have become involved with the martial art aikido. Derived from a blending of numerous martial art systems, it means the method or way (do), for the coordination or harmony (ai), of mental or spirit energy (ki). Once again, I am challenged to develop my intuition. I must "learn it" (aikido) by heart. There is no time to "think" and analyze on the mat, as the defender (nage) must instinctively respond to the attacker's (uke's) challenge; the response is one of blending and trust, a relationship formed out of caring and love. The dojo (where one practices aikido) is also a place of love and I can't define why. I just intuitively feel that way and that's all I need. I have learned to trust my instincts and move in the direction of emotional independence. Such are the advantages of being intuitive and practicing aikido.

The *Tao Te Ching*, too, strongly encourages you to cultivate inner knowledge—the intuitive self. When your inner self reflects the outer world, alignment with nature is achieved. You are then in a position to achieve joy and fulfillment.

John Heider's *Tao of Leadership* suggests that you cultivate your instincts by not pushing or trying to figure things out. "When you cannot see what is happening relax and look with your inner eye. When you do not understand, listen; when you are puzzled, become calm; to know what's happening, use intuition."

You have unlimited amounts of potential and information available when you choose to tap into this vast storehouse. Whether confronted with a major crisis, stressed by a major decision or problem, or simply looking for an alternative to everyday, mundane realities, your inner voice is there to help matters work out. It is your most reliable guide.

Logic is based on the known; go beyond this limit to unlimited pastures of the unknown—your unlimited intuition.

As I write this, I recall an incident that recently happened as a result of following a new path, literally and figuratively. Walking into town, I had a strong, intuitive feeling to go out of my way and take a route different from my usual direct path. I listened to my inner voice and, as I turned the "new" corner, I came upon a man who was flat on his back next to the curb. I rushed to help; he was having a seizure. I asked someone to call an ambulance and the police. It all worked out well. As if this weren't intuitive enough, the previous night I had had a dream in which I discovered the body of a man, dead in the street. Fortunately that is not exactly what happened. Coincidence? Perhaps, but I do believe there was something metaphysical taking place. The mind is an amazing phenomenon, understood by few people. But that shouldn't stop you from using it.

CHAPTER ELEVEN

BEYOND LIMITED EXCELLENCE: THE ULTIMATE EXPERIENCE

Perfection belongs to the gods; the most that we can hope for is excellence.

Carl Jung

EXCELLENCE AND THE WAY OF NATURE

I have been sitting at my desk for forty-five minutes trying to capture your attention with the perfect opening to this section; I have a severe case of writer's block. Not a word of wisdom has been recorded, and my wastebasket is becoming inundated with pages of rejected attempts to write the perfect sentence. I can't help but recall the eloquence of Mark Twain who said, "The difference between the right word and the almost right word is the difference between lightning and the lightning bug." I want to dazzle you with the right word—none of that "almost" nonsense for me. Being the perfect writer I am, I'm fearful that you'll reject what I write until it's perfect. Sound familiar? The problem is, waiting for the right word or thought to appear could take me forever, and this book would never be completed. I often wonder why I let the fear of being criticized for being less than perfect interfere with the joy of doing the task.

Have you ever experienced being immobilized in the present out of fear you'll be judged imperfect in the future? It happened often in my past until I came across a bumper sticker as I sat in heavy traffic one hot afternoon: "LIFE'S NOT PERFECT, GET IT DONE." Talk about making my day? Instant joy! These few words changed my life dramatically. I now continue to "begin," without constant concern for being perfect at everything. *I have addressed my addiction to perfection.* I feel free once again, and very gratified that perfection doesn't rule my life at all times.

Taking the advice of Carl Jung in the introductory quote, rather than perfection, I seek a path of excellence when possible. My search for perfection has caused too much pain, anxiety, stress and frustration. How unfulfilling! The pursuit of perfection represents total misalignment with the law of nature. According to nature's way, the belief that you can be perfect is a self-imposed illusion that seriously limits your potential for happiness, and since it is unattainable, such a quest by itself is a lethal imperfection. Pursuing the impossible is an imperfect act. The *Tao Te Ching* explains how the efforts to be perfect are, indeed, limiting. To continue this unhealthy pursuit is to place yourself and the world around you into constant strife and disharmony. The Tao's concept of *wu wei*, once again, is very appropriate. The search for perfection is an attempt to "force" what can't be, to control that which can't be controlled. The Tao teaches us to let go and flow, but for the perfectionist, this is to be "out of control." What I notice when I let go, however, is a paradoxical reaction: In *releasing* the need to be one hundred percent perfect, I receive what I want. With the pressure to be perfect put aside, I do excellent work, often exceeding limits that I thought were mine.

PERFECTION: THE LEARNED ADDICTION

Let's face it—the world admires perfection. Everyone loves the perfect host, the perfect dinner and the perfect home. Magazines and television espouse perfect hair, perfect teeth, perfect complexions, perfect bodies. Blemishes are abominable, to be avoided at all costs. No wonder we all fall into the perfectionist trap. Dr. Baila Zeitz, a psychologist who conducted a study with the New York City Center for Research on women's careers, states that growing up female in today's society leads women to conclude that "in order to achieve at their careers, they have to be twice as good as men." Thus, we conclude that perfection is the only sure way to advancement in our sexist world. Such attitudes carry over, for example, into the field of athletics in which women constantly have to prove their worth to the public. The need to justify their existence in the same arena as men induces enormous pressure to be the perfect athlete. Of course, women don't have a monopoly on perfectionism; we are all limited by such attitudes, whether you are a perfectionist, or just live or work with one. It is the gold medal olympians who get the attention; all the rest are "losers" in a society that extols the merits of perfection.

As with most psychological addictions, perfectionism is learned. It keeps you spellbound. The payoffs are great yet short-lived, making you ravenous for another "fix." Psychologists refer to perfectionism as an *obsessive-compulsive behavior* that drives you constantly to do better and better. However, you never feel quite fulfilled despite a series of "perfect" 10's on your gymnastic routines, straight A's in school or compliments from your boss. There will always be that critic in the mind that focuses on your slightest, unobservable mistake.

If you were to trace such attitudes back to their origin, you would discover that the motivation to be perfect arises out of an acute and childhood-based need for approval from others. Perhaps the early years were spent in a critical environment where love was withheld until perfection was attained. Dr. David Burns, a Philadelphia psychiatrist and researcher in the area of perfectionism, agrees and points out that perfectionists are so afraid of rejection, they usually take criticism badly. Their reaction to criticism alienates others and brings about the disapproval they fear. This behavior pattern only serves to strengthen the belief that in order to win approval they must be perfect. According to Burns, love, respect and reward are theirs only if the perfectionists are bigger, better and more wonderful than they actually can be.

THE IMPERFECT QUEST

In his book, Feeling Good: The New Mood Therapy, Burns talks about perfectionism as being "the world's greatest con" game. It's a concept that doesn't fit reality and fails to blend with "the way." It does, however, fit a distorted set of beliefs that perfectionists have of themselves. In a sense, they do become perfect—perfect at being discontented. Perhaps they should strive for just being normal, since "normal" people seem to be at ease. To exert yourself and believe you can achieve perfection may be the greatest illusion of a lifetime. The desire for perfection, says Frenchman Louis Fontanes, is the worst disease that ever afflicted the human mind. And, as William Shakespeare so eloquently stated, "No perfection is so absolute that some impurity does not pollute."

The implications of these thoughts, for all of us, are astounding. The pursuit of perfection seriously hampers our quest for joy and fulfillment. Better to focus on achieving excellence, a more worthwhile, joyful, achievable and less stressful goal. Yet it's often difficult to distinguish between the healthy journey of excellence and the stress-laden, addictive pursuit of perfection. Detecting which direction you are taking is the first step to creating positive change. The following chart contains some guidelines that will help you determine which side of the fence you are on.

Pursuit of Excellence	Search for Perfection
1) Striving for high standards	1) Attaining goals as sole result
2) Internal rewards	2) External rewards
3) Self-satisfaction	3) Satisfaction only from others' opinions
4) Flexible, realistic goals	4) Rigid, unattainable goals
5) Can risk failure and learn	5) Failure is intolerable
6) Focus on the positive outcomes	6) Dwelling on the negative outcomes
7) Average performance is okay	7) "All perfect or nothing doing" thinking
8) Emphasis on *how* the game is played	8) Emphasis on the outcome only
9) Go ahead under imperfect conditions	9) Procrastinate until all conditions are perfect
10) Sense of self-worth just by *doing*	10) Self-worth equated with end result/accomplishment
11) Joy of competition	11) Fear of failure
12) Feel disappointed in outcomes	12) Feel disappointed in who I am

TO ACT ACCORDINGLY

LIFE IS A ROLLER COASTER
Perhaps the only predictable aspect of life is the knowledge that *change is inevitable.* Changes and cycles are constant. According to the Tao, nature balances extremes through cold and hot, wet and dry, depending upon the time of year when change is meant to happen. Like the seasons of nature, you, too, have rhythms and passages. Things come and go, and to fight or resist these patterns is to cause unnecessary

stress and inner turmoil. Life is, indeed, a roller coaster ride and requires the ability to flow. Careers, family, friends, homes and finances are equally affected by constant change. Even the determined perfectionist is a "victim" of nature's process of change. However, the perfectionist sees any variation from what "should be" as a grave mishap, a casualty, calamity or stroke of misfortune. Such dreadful experiences are to be conquered, never to happen again. He believes he can control the wavering force of nature and will only act when he can be sure things will turn out as they "should be." This means he must be thoroughly competent, achieving and successful in every aspect of life.

I was recently talking with a client, a youthful high school English teacher who believed she could live up to such irrational, unrealistic expectations. This was the source of her enormous stress and anxiety. These attitudes alone would result in her sabotaging her efforts to be the perfect professional, guaranteeing a sub-par performance.

To reduce this tension and change the belief, we used a technique called "cognitive restructuring": What you feel is the result of how you view a situation; change the view and the feelings (tension, anxiety) will change. We explored the fact that the road to success is a roller coaster. It was impossible for her to be "right on" every day, particularly during her first year on the job. Ups and downs are to be expected. I related to her an example from the field of sports: Babe Ruth hit many home runs, yet *he struck out 1,373 times!* She began to change her view about what to expect from herself. I mentioned that no one escapes setbacks. As a matter of fact, mistakes can be a teacher and act as a natural aspect of the growth process. In the words of the Samurai warrior, "Expect nothing and be ready for anything." One day you are fantastic, and the next you'll ponder leaving the profession. Everyone experiences these swings. She began to realize that her belief was irrational, and, like all performers and achievers, she would continue to experience fluctuations on the road to excellence. She learned to not take herself so seriously and to focus on the students as people who could help her become the excellent teacher she wants to be. In this way, her ego became less of an issue as she related more with her heart.

This lesson has valuable implications for everyday living, as well. Much of the turmoil, stress, anxiety and frustration in our relationships comes from our irrational belief that we can be competent and successful at all times. Not only are perfectionists affected by such unrealistic expectations, but those who work and live with them experience emotional havoc and pain as well. Life is a series of ups and downs, errors and mistakes, advances and retreats. We need to align ourselves with nature's way and accept this reality if we are to experience improved performance and fulfillment.

SUCCESS IS TAKING THE RISK

Part of the motivation underlying perfectionistic behavior is the fear of failure (see the chapter on courage). The possibility of failure, with its accompanying disapproval from others, is a frightening prospect and leads to paralysis or immobilization. When there's so much to lose, why take the chance? The belief that people will approve of you if you're perfect is another one of those irrational beliefs, because even after an outstanding performance, some will be envious of your success and find it difficult to be positive and share your enthusiasm.

Risk-taking becomes a "self-worth" issue. Perfectionists learn early on to equate self-worth with achievement. Therefore, they will shun participation in any event where failure is possible. In a sense, they become immobilized. In the words of Winston Churchill, "the maxim 'nothing avails but perfection' may be spelled PARALYSIS." Out of fear of being less than perfect, they resist "doing." Procrastination is now the issue, and all goes "on hold" until the perfect time arrives; but of course it never comes. Aiming for perfection all the time is an endless foray into the forest of frustration.

169

To help people take risks, I use a process of redefining what failure *really* is. I suggest that holding back out of *fear* of failure means you never attain the goal and *this is failure*. However, if you take the risk, you will either be instantly successful or experience a setback from which you will learn and increase your chances for a success at a later time. If the goal is realistic, you will eventually reach your objective. Success, therefore, is the ability to take the risk, learn from errors and setbacks, and forge ahead. Self-worth can now be measured by the willingness to "do" regardless of the outcome. Such a change in attitude will enable you eventually to reach your destination.

SATISFACTION IS CRUCIAL

Since perfectionism creates enormous pressure, tension, anxiety and frustration, it becomes almost impossible to experience joy and satisfaction. When the joy in any activity ceases to exist, excellence is difficult to obtain. All-Star Pete Rose, of the Cincinnati Reds, once commented on "excellent play" by alluding to the joy he had received from the game. So many prominent athletes play because it's satisfying and joyfully rewarding. The solution to the perfectionist's problem is to recapture the romance and passion with the *process* of achieving rather than just with the final outcome. Concentrating on the pleasure and satisfaction you receive from your endeavor will reduce the pressures and ultimately enhance performance.

A top-level corporate executive client of mine was having much difficulty with her staff. She was an "impossible to please" perfectionist, always trying to exert control. The more perfection she demanded, the more they "rebelled" with inferior work. Anxiety, tension and fear became obstacles standing in the way of success. Everyone was miserable.

She wondered if she needed to hire new people. I told her that the real culprit was probably the controlling environment she was creating. "Is anyone having any fun or enjoyment? What is satisfying about the job?" I asked. She began to see, after some introspective sessions, that she was losing perspective on all the great wonders of her job and also that she pushed and forced her distorted view upon the rest of the staff.

A meeting was held among all parties to discuss a new direction, a new focus, one that emphasized joy, pleasure and cooperation, with a minimum of control. There was a rebirth of enthusiasm and a resurgence in performance for everyone. Their theme is now one of "excellence with joy and satisfaction"; she reports that the new criteria for performance saved the day. Everyone now seems quite satisfied.

The *Tao Te Ching* speaks so eloquently about coercive leaders who force, push or manipulate their workers into doing what's right or perfect. The more one tries to control, the more resistant the group will become. Lao Tzu believed that too many controls produce rebellion among workers and interfere with the natural processes of group cohesion and spirit. The wise leader will establish a climate of openness and spontaneity with less emphasis on regulations for perfection. The group will then blossom and act accordingly, with joy and harmony. Work will prosper when force and control, for the purposes of perfection, diminish.

WINNING IS UNI-DIMENSIONAL

One of the major characteristics of the perfectionist is an obsession with the final score. The finish line, a bid on a contract or a routine argument at home are all criteria for *winning* as the only success. John Wooden, former coach of the UCLA Bruins basketball dynasty, knows something about winning. After dominating the collegiate basketball scene for fifteen years, he stated that winning "breeds envy and distrust in others, and overconfidence and a lack of appreciation in those who enjoy it." This seems to hold up in everyday situations as well. Respected professionals, athletes and other achievers are beginning to reevaluate traditional attitudes toward winning. The outcome of an event or situation represents one small aspect of the total experience; excellence goes deeper than the ephemeral numbers on the scoreboard.

I recently experienced working with a female gymnast who believed that "winning was the only thing." She was terribly depressed after a recent loss (second place) to a rival university opponent, and she exhibited this by signs of anger, weeping and self-imposed isolation. She saw excellence in performance as an outcome rather than as a process. In this case, it was necessary to coordinate my suggestions with those of her coach in order to maximize her chances of personal satisfaction with the process as well as joy in the end results. We talked about measuring success by the mastery of certain skills and routines, rather than the final score in competition. The coach agreed to support these realistic goals as well as judging her performance over a period of time rather than by the outcome of a few events. I also asked her to develop some affirmation (see chapter on affirmations) that would reinforce process rather than outcome. For example, she would say over and over: "I may not win the event but I perform like a champion." Our choice of words, as you now know, has an incredibly powerful impact on performance.

In addition to suggesting this affirmation, I asked her to list all the positive and negative aspects of trying to be perfect. On the positive side, she listed that it feels good to come close to perfection and actually win; however, the negative column of her ledger was filled with entries that were the source of much stress, pressure, anxiety and frustration. It quickly became apparent that perfectionism is not "cost-effective"; thus, changing became easier for her. The quest for perfection is a uni-dimensional act with a perfect end result being the only satisfaction. The one-dimensional approach lacks the rich, expansive experience that life can bring us when we risk, try and "go for it," whatever the result.

ALTER YOUR GAME PLAN

I often encounter the confirmed perfectionist who claims that without this personal addiction, he wouldn't be as successful; he couldn't do it without it. I immediately respond, "How do you know; have you ever altered your approach?" Perhaps you are successful in spite of your perfectionistic tendencies but—think about this—you *might* be *even better* without them. Take the risk!

For example, I have a tendency to over-prepare lectures, seminars and classes; I visualize, rehearse and practice the content and delivery until it's "perfectly" smooth (which, of course, it never is). I've had success with this method and attribute such positive results to my excessive conscientiousness; yet much time and energy are involved. As recently as yesterday I was confronted with a near-panic situation. I was scheduled to give a three-hour seminar at a local university and, because of an enormous amount of pressing work and prior commitments, I left the preparation of that class to the last minute. Forced to alter my usual compulsive "game plan," I arrived with only forty minutes of preparation and gave a performance that went *well beyond* what I ever would have expected using my "old" techniques.

So I've learned a valuable lesson within the last twenty-four hours: Relax, prepare and risk not having the perfect performance. I put it to the test and all went "beyond" belief. Doing less, strangely enough, sometimes produces more. Using my thoughts on COURAGE, I plan to take the risk and prepare for upcoming stressful events in a less perfectionistic way. The reduction in pressure should positively influence performance.

ASSESS PROFIT AND LOSS

I ask you to notice, like the gymnast in the previous section, those times you tend to be perfectionistic, and, in two columns, list the pros and cons of such behavior. What do you gain by being a perfectionist? What do you lose? There's a good chance that your standards for perfection are of no benefit; the emotional, social and mental upheaval that result are stiff prices to pay in light of the few, if any, profits.

This listing of pros and cons is a simple yet powerful way to expose the truth. It's a method that can be commonly and effectively used for assessing the pluses or minuses of any situation relating to careers, relationships, changing locations, problems or decisions of any kind. Think about such mundane events as tennis, bowling, cleaning, ironing or cooking. Simply use this "pro and con" approach and notice that the world is no worse off for you having just tried—and had fun doing it. Think of how much aggravation you could eliminate by just "doing," and not "doing the best." Happy days are here again ... for all involved.

SOME MAXIMS TO PONDER

Finally, for those moments when you need a quick reminder to avoid the perfectionist trap, consider the following:

> Applaud the setting of less ambitious goals. They also feel good.
>
> We live in a world where nobody can be perfect, so strive for excellence.
>
> Error is a factor that is always with us. Learn from it.
>
> True perfection only exists when one dies.
>
> It is natural to be imperfect; that's what we are. Join the human race.
>
> Every failure is an opportunity to grow.
>
> Everything can be improved upon if you look at it from every angle.

THE BALANCE

The key to working successfully to overcome perfection-orientation is to maintain balance. Balance is the pursuit of *excellence*, the striving for certain standards in your approach to things you do, rather than concern for just the outcome. The process involves searching for internal awards and rewards based on flexible, realistic goals. Emphasize *how* the game is played, not just end results. Although you may occasionally feel disappointed in the results, never internalize them as a commentary on *who you are.*

Studies with olympic athletes have shown that those with balance, those who pursue excellence, have better chances of making the team than those who set unrealistic, perfectionistic goals. I notice this to be true in all aspects of life, and especially in sports, which are a microcosm of universal reality. The same principles apply to the corporate structure, family life and spiritual-emotional endeavors.

Without balance, you are denied the opportunity to risk, grow, change and to live a life of optimal potential. You will be controlled by fear if you attempt to control an uncontrollable world.

The bottom line? Perfection is a dead end; it places you in a losing *Catch-22* battle. If people recognize your great work, you'll worry about meeting those high standards next time around. If you fail in their eyes, you'll be devastated. Either way, you'll be anxious and tense. It's the perfect "NO-WIN" situation, and that's about as close as you'll get to perfection!

I feel as if this chapter is far from perfect, yet in light of what I've been writing about, perhaps this is the best possible example of balance. I did thoroughly enjoy writing it once I finally began, and I feel quite satisfied and know that it will give all of us food for thought and possibilities for change. I've tried to be perfect too often, and the result has been burnout and boredom. I don't want to fall into the trap of striving for perfection at this late date. Remember, the Tao emphasizes BALANCE; it is the doorway to fulfillment. Besides, in the words of W. Somerset Maugham, "Perfection has one great defect—it's apt to be dull"; and dull I do not wish to be. For once, let us all put to rest this great, addictive, *limiting illusion.*

CHAPTER TWELVE

BEYOND LIMITED BALANCE: THE ULTIMATE SELF.

The way of Nature, in step with the Tao, is considered the ideal in behavior...Nothing escapes the laws of Nature. The Tao in Nature is intelligent and powerful...it responds to potentially unbalancing extremes with precision and accuracy.

R. L. Wing
The Tao of Power

BALANCE AND THE WAY OF NATURE

This is the age of specialization. So much pressure is exerted upon us to narrow our focus and concentrate on one small aspect of what we do. Recognition as "the expert" in a particular area of choice is rewarding and gratifying, yet it is not without its drawbacks. The field of dentistry is a perfect example; thirty years ago, one doctor did it all—cleaned teeth, filled cavities and did the extraction, root canal and gum work. You name it, he did it. Today, you could conceivably be involved with four dental experts as a result of one problem. Now, I realize that this is the most efficient and effective way to bring excellent care to the patient, yet I wonder how this affects the well-being and motivation of the doctor. Could one really do root canals in machine-like fashion for the next twenty-five years and still relate to patients as people? How fulfilling could that be? The *Tao Te Ching* refers to the possible limits of specialization: Those who specialize seem to put an end to creativity and cease to evolve. People and organizations that focus too narrowly create an imbalance and risk burnout. The Tao would encourage one to create more of a balance in life outside the workplace, a balance of physical, social, spiritual and familial activities to "round out" the experience in life and prevent possible "extinction" of these wonderful aspects of life. So many of us grow tired of activities we initially love because there's not enough variety in what we do. There's much wisdom attached to the adage: "variety is the spice of life." It seems to be the joy, the raison d'être, the element that makes things happen.

A pediatric cardiologist friend of mine spends an enormous amount of time each day with life and death situations. Each case may vary slightly but the theme is the same: SURVIVAL. Fortunately, John scuba dives, pilots his own plane, cycles, runs and surfs when time permits. Because of his extracurricular activities, he is a better physician.

I work with many people who are severely depressed because their life is too uni-dimensional. They are paying an exorbitant fee for putting all their eggs in one basket.

The lack of balance and how it affects one's life is easily understood by observing the reactions of olympic athletes at the completion of their long, arduous journey toward the "gold." Rewarding as the outcome may be, how does the intense, narrowly focused lifestyle affect the development of these stars, particularly the younger ones? In the recent Olympiad, one of the champion swimmers was asked, "Where do you go from here?" The response was instantaneous: "Far away from pools." He vowed to avoid swimming in a pool for the next two years. He proceeded to relate how much was sacrificed on his road to fame and intimated that it might not have been worth it. He felt that the lack of balance in his life had contributed to his feelings; yet because of this narrow focus he was able to reach great heights.

As an achiever myself, I have often experienced the absence of balance. There have been periods when I've been obsessed with competitive running while totally excluding everything else. I also have become so self-absorbed in my work at times that I ignored my family and friends. And then there have been moments in which I would just play, day after day, and do a good job at it. Other aspects of my reality, however, were put on hold. I "succeeded" at what I did, yet I knew something was lost in the process. I still felt a void—something was missing. My lopsided, asymmetrical existence was not as fulfilling as I thought it would be. I am presently creating a balance in my life between body, mind and emotions, and it feels terrific. Best of all, I've learned that I can still be good at what I do; *balance and excellence are compatible partners.* Actually, I believe that because of the balance, excellence is more attainable. Those who seem to do the best in their field, the people I most admire, are those who have established a wonderful "evenness" to their personal, social, home and community lives.

This brings us to another principle of nature that, when followed, will enhance the possibilities for personal joy and happiness. It states that *the extent of one's fulfillment in life is the direct result of the balance created among the physical, mental and emotional-spiritual selves.* Failure to attend to all components creates a void that will restrain total wellness and joy. Concentrating only on any one in particular produces an extreme, an imbalance with the way of nature. By following the teachings of the Tao, extremes can be avoided while you gain personal power through moderation. The *Tao Te Ching* can assist you in your attempts to become aware of extremes and restore the balance. The Tao, itself, is the balance; you just need to notice that.

TO ACT ACCORDINGLY

The process of creating BALANCE in life is no different from the way one balances a diet. Good nutrition means that the body is presented with the right combination of carbohydrates, fats and proteins, whose amounts vary depending upon the individual's needs. So it is with life. You function more effectively, and experience greater overall wellness, when the balance among the BODY, MIND and SPIRIT is established. As with a diet, such synchronicity is possible only when you keep a constant vigil; you must always notice other patterns you follow and correct for error when drifting off course.

Being successful in maintaining the BALANCE has less to do with how good you are or how hard you work at it than it does with the ability to go beyond the self-imposed limit of TIME. Many people believe there isn't enough time to "do it all." I would immediately refer them to Chapter Four on beliefs. There is plenty of time; you just have to learn to use it more efficiently. For example, I recently learned that I function quite well on seven hours of sleep each night. I go to bed at ten, get up at five and write until seven-thirty a.m. By the end of a month, I will have logged an extra seventy-five hours, enough to finish several chapters of this book. I'll write later in this chapter about how to get the time you need. For now, let's consider some ways to bring balance to our lives.

EMOTIONAL-SPIRITUAL SELF

Since the early 1980s, we have witnessed a proliferation of interest in personal consciousness and spirituality. Within the next five years, I predict this movement will reach the business world and corporate structure, with a strong focus on inner self-development (INTUITIVE MANAGEMENT, balance, process-orientation and more). The whole country is beginning to discover what the Eastern philosophies have taught for centuries: A life of fulfillment, achievement and productivity calls for serious inner work, the exploration of the expanding frontiers of human consciousness and ways in which to use this "new" information for a more balanced, productive life.

Because of this rapidly growing movement, emotional-spiritual growth possibilities are readily available. Churches and religions have been with us from time immemorial. They still play an important role in many people's lives. Today, however, more options seem to be available for those seeking a less structured, more personal journey based on the wisdom of many different religions, spiritual practices and philosophies.

The availability of books on these subjects, such as the one you are reading, is an indication of what's wanted by the public as well as publishing companies' commitment to meeting that need. There are bookstores in most big cities throughout this country whose entire stock is reflective of the "new age," Eastern philosophical, metaphysical genre. Such reading is not only stimulating but helpful in the formulation of an applied personal spiritual path.

In addition to reading material, there's a whole new wave of music that has flooded the market: sounds that facilitate inner reflection, peace and spiritual thought. Such beautiful music is a wonderful adjunct to meditation, relaxation, reading and communication between friends.

Depending upon your geographical location, there may be group seminars available for the purpose of pursuing spiritual growth and change. The many formats often require a weekend commitment of intense training. In California, you can be like "a kid in a candy store"; there's something going on every week, for instance, in the San Francisco Bay area alone.

There is, however, no need to spend large sums of money to become balanced; this could actually be just another "extreme" in disguise. Real spiritual growth starts inside and ripples outward. Begin with you and your family; bring joy and love to your home. This is the most important step toward the development of a strong spiritual self.

And don't discount the power of laughter and humor in the creation of a balance; they are nature's best antidote for pain, fear, depression and physical illness. Norman Cousins has written volumes about the benefits of humor to a healthy life. I personally recommend his books, *The Healing Heart* and *Anatomy of an Illness*.

PHYSICAL SELF

Many of us overlook the physical aspects of the creation of personal balance, which include both exercise and nutrition.

Exercise. The most frequently used reason why people fail to incorporate exercise into their lives is lack of time. I always say, "Either you pay now or you pay later." People who don't exercise vigorously are more prone to degenerative disease, which takes time away in later years as sickness strikes. In any case, taking time to exercise now is money in the bank with high interest rates. You get about a three for one return on your investment: three hours of high-energy productivity for every hour of exercise. So you actually save time. What you accomplish in those three hours might normally take five; you're ahead one hour.

To make the most of the time-crunch of my busy schedule, I always carry a bag of running gear with me on the plane. Recently I experienced a four-hour layover in Salt Lake City, Utah; I changed in the men's room, placed my clothes in a convenient locker, and ran through the terminal and out of the airport into the big city. I returned after sixteen miles, washed off with a sponge, changed clothes and reduced my wait to only forty-five minutes. There's always time. You just have to notice.

All you need do to maintain excellent fitness is to work out aerobically (see Ken Cooper's book, *The New Aerobics*) for thirty consecutive minutes, three to four times a week. Walking, swimming, running, skiing, skating and cycling are a few of the more popular routes to take. If you feel self-conscious, or the weather is atrocious, working out on exercise cycles and indoor rowing machines accomplishes the same goal.

Exercise creates a sense of internal harmony among the mind, body and all of its systems; it feels terrific. Your relationship with yourself will improve, as will productivity at work. Running has provided me with many hours of creative thought. I put together in my mind the outline for this book during a very long run in the peaceful forest that surrounds my home.

These desirable aspects of aerobic exercise are just the "tip of the iceberg" with respect to all of the accompanying benefits. The following physiological gains are also available to anyone involved in a consistent training program. Use these as motivators to encourage you to maintain a healthy physical self.

BLOOD PRESSURE LOWERS. With regular exercise, you experience increased vessel size and elasticity, the major factors involved in decreased blood pressure.

BLOOD QUALITY RISES. Through exercise, there is an increase in the number of blood cells, as well as more hemoglobin and more plasma (the liquid portion of blood). Also, the blood's ability to dissolve clots will improve.

HIGH-DENSITY LIPOPROTEIN LEVELS RISE. HDL's apparently help clear the arteries of unhealthy cholesterol deposits. Regular aerobic exercise raises the level of HDL's in the blood, thus intensifying the clearing process.

HEART GETS STRONGER. Like any muscle, the heart will

grow larger and stronger if it's worked. Exercising regularly will help the heart to become more efficient and effective.

LUNGS BECOME MORE EFFICIENT. When you work the lungs through aerobic exercise, they open up and flush out, using more air space. Exercise also helps to reduce the effects of asthma and emphysema.

MUSCLE TONE IMPROVES. Your body begins to look aesthetically more appealing as muscles take on better tone and definition.

OSTEOPOROSIS IS CONTROLLED. This condition results from too severe a decrease in bone density, causing weaker bones to fracture. Exercise seems to delay or even reverse this possibility.

WEIGHT IS CONTROLLED. Exercise speeds up metabolism, decreases the appetite and burns fat.

GASTRO-INTESTINAL SYSTEM BENEFITS. The G-I tract becomes more efficient as exercise increases the motility of the intestines.

AGING IS DELAYED. Although more research is needed, it seems as though the above benefits help exercise buffs to age less quickly than their sedentary counterparts.

THOUGHT PROCESSES ARE ENHANCED. Some studies indicate improvement in decision-making capability in subjects who exercised vigorously on a regular basis.

CREATIVITY IS ENCOURAGED. Although it's highly subjective data, some people report that exercising facilitates the flow of ideas and thoughts.

STRESS IS CONTROLLED. Probably one of the most irrefutable physiological benefits of exercise is that it is one of the most satisfying means of stress reduction.

CHRONIC TIREDNESS IS REDUCED. Exercise stimulates the circulatory system, transporting an abundance of oxygen that enables you to remain alert and awake.

DEGENERATIVE DISEASES ARE CONTROLLED. Regular aerobic activity makes you less vulnerable to such diseases as diabetes, cancer, heart failure and arthritis.

Diet. There is so much contradictory evidence on the topic of nutrition as to what's important for a healthy diet. Such confusion leads to discouragement and an attitude of "who cares?" I'm no expert on the subject, and what is good for me may not be good for you. However, I do know of some universally accepted "truths" that most reasonably aware nutritionists would pass along. These should at least give you a start in the right direction.

The bottom line to the creation of harmony with nature is not only to eat a balanced diet but to eat one that's free of poisons, additives and artificial or processed foods. If you owned an expensive car, you would never consider putting "junk food" oil or gas into it; why would you not apply this rule for a body that's worth so much more and can't ever be replaced?

The following dietary options can improve weight control, immune response, self-esteem and overall wellness:

> less red meat
> fewer dairy foods
> less sugar
> less salt
> less alcohol, coffee and chocolate
> more fresh vegetables
> more fruit
> more whole grains
> more pure water
> moderation in eating, at all times

MENTAL SELF

Daily conscious attempts to use the mind in a positive way are crucial to the process of balance. I recommend any form of meditation whereby you create quiet time alone to slow down and silence the endless stream of "mind chatter." There are many ways to "travel within" that will help you to "travel about" in a more harmonious, centered way. Some people prefer to think of "nothing," while others focus upon specific concerns in order to attain greater clarity for resolving personal issues. For me, running in the woods or along the ocean is a wonderful opportunity to meditate, as the hypnotic cadence puts me into a quiet trance. I know of people who, in the stillness of the early morning, sit and gaze at the flame of a candle. Starting the day in this way can prepare you to cope more effectively with the onslaught of ensuing pressures.

Whatever form you choose, remember that the benefits of giving to yourself in this way are far-reaching, too numerous to count. However, you must be consistent, with at least fifteen minutes a day of practice. You will not benefit by trying to do it all in two hours on a Sunday.

In addition to the meditation process, PLAY is another way to attend to the mind. Like a child, you need to include time to rekindle your excitement, enthusiasm and perspective. You know best how to do this; I leave it up to you. Aimless playfulness is part of the balance.

CREATING MORE TIME

There are only twenty-four hours in a day. How could you possibly squeeze another five minutes from your hectic schedule? You don't need to do any squeezing. If you do, something is not right—your life is not working. What needs to be done is a reevaluation of how you proportion your time and how you can reduce the clutter and unnecessary distractions. I have had much success, both personally and with my clients, using the following TIME MANIPULATORS.

Extra Day a Month. You can "buy" at least an extra day a month if you go to bed a half-hour earlier and wake up thirty minutes before scheduled. Forget the ten o'clock news; it doesn't change that much, and the violence reported raises your level of anxiety, which interferes with restful sleep. Most of us get more sleep than we need. Examine your belief about how much sleep you think is necessary; ,perhaps you can go beyond your perceived limit.

Fill the "Dead" Time. You spend an enormous amount of time waiting: You pause for red lights, wait for trains and planes; you're put "on hold" in doctor's offices; you become delayed by undependable friends who forget the meaning of punctuality. What do you do in the interim? These are valuable moments that can turn into hours. By taking reading material with me wherever I go, I manage to read an extra two books a month just during the waiting time. This contributes to my well-being and reduces the stress and negativity attached to such "dead" time. I no longer become annoyed since my time is well spent; waiting is an enjoyable, fulfilling part of my day.

By the way, if you commute alone in a car, consider making use of the down-time by playing language or self-growth tapes; learn as the wheels turn.

Prioritize. I often become overwhelmed by the amount of work that needs to get finished. This creates much anxiety and, as a result, nothing gets done. Or I spend an inordinate amount of time on projects that could wait and fail to meet deadlines for the urgent jobs. To help save time, I put tasks in the order of URGENT, IMPORTANT and NON-ESSENTIAL. I focus on the urgent during my most productive time of day (for me, the morning hours). Once these are completed, I take half of the important tasks, work with them and leave the rest for another day. I repeat the process each day; what's non-essential today may become urgent next week. I prioritize one day at a time and go with the flow. Things change daily and I want to act (react) accordingly.

Daily Dozen. To maintain a daily balance, each night I draw up a list of twelve items related to body, mind and spirit that

I'd like to accomplish the following day. The groups of goals will typically include running, reading, writing, meditating, cooking, playing with the family, working with clients or any other activity that contributes to a harmonious day. As they come to pass, I proudly check off each objective; this becomes a positive reinforcer that contributes to the development of balanced habit formation. Being so organized also helps to free up extra time since no minutes are wasted. Don't hesitate to put "doing nothing" as a goal. This may be more difficult than it appears, but it is worth the effort. Emptiness, according to the Taoists, is another part of the balance. To have a complete, full schedule is an extreme to be avoided.

Learn to Say NO. Bosses, friends and family can be very demanding at times, without even realizing it. In your attempt to please others or win approval, you say yes to their requests and hold resentment when they become impositions. Your time becomes "confiscated," and an imbalance is created as your daily goals get put on hold. Over a period of time, failure to say "no" creates much unhappiness and inner turmoil.

The key to declining outside requests in a productive way is *communication*. Simply saying, "No, I can't," leaves the situation open to many interpretations like: "I can't, now; I'm not able to; I never want to; I'd like to but I'm afraid; I'd love to another time." Information is missing.

The other day, for example, I was invited to a dinner party and responded by saying, "What a great idea—thanks; I wish I could come but I have plans for that night. I'd love to do it some other time, though." My message could not be misinterpreted; I filled in the blanks, precluding any misunderstanding.

Then there are those moments when a demand is placed upon me and I want no part of it. I receive the respect of that person by simply saying, "No, I don't feel comfortable with that." For the insensitive, unconscious boss who fails to consider your world, say that you'd be able to accomplish that but other requests have been made prior to his; you will get to it in sequence. You may even ask this person for some help in resolving your dilemma.

The point is: Don't assume you need to act upon all that comes your way. A quiet *no*, spoken with a smile, often gives you what you deserve: control over your life with extra time to meet your own needs.

Power to the People. Many of us have difficulty empowering others to do certain jobs that we believe can only be done by us. This is the "only one right way" attitude to which many perfectionists become attached. Such an inflexible, rigid stance is another limiting, time-consuming belief that needs to be examined. If others volunteer to do your work, let them. You may be a better cook, a faster typist or a more eloquent report writer, but someone else can do a "good enough" job. The immediate outcome of "letting go" is the creation of more personal time to create the balance. See Chapter Eleven for more on perfectionistic tendencies.

Repeated throughout the *Tao Te Ching* is the notion of using nature to balance extremes in the world rather than causing them. The foregoing discussion as well as your intuitive mind (Chapter Ten) are wonderful tools to help you tune into what's needed to create the balance. Notice the times when you have a food craving. This is your body's way of balancing its needs. Children and animals are good at knowing instinctively what's needed. They act upon the world without unbalancing it. We just need to trust our minds and heart . . . to listen, and when we get a strong urge to be physical, mental or spiritual, act accordingly. You have the power to neutralize extremes if you follow those feelings. Lao Tzu believed that this is not only possible but necessary, if you are to make sense out of your world.

CHAPTER THIRTEEN

BEYOND LIMITED LOVE: THE ULTIMATE GIFT

When the night has been too lonely
and the road has been too long;
And you think that love is only
For the lucky and the strong,
Just remember in the winter,
Far beneath the bitter snow,
Lies the seed that with the sun's love,
In the spring becomes the rose.

Amanda McBroom
"The Rose"

LOVE AND THE WAY OF NATURE

As a recipient of a doctoral degree in psychology from a major university, I have been exposed to a wide variety of professional courses pertaining to the mind and emotions. These required an in-depth understanding of most human concerns such as anger, depression, fear, frustration, sorrow, panic, anxiety and other related disturbances. However, as I contemplate that education process years later, I realize that

189

all the texts, seminars, lectures and clinical experiences curiously avoided the most powerful ingredient to help people work through and resolve so many of these painful reactions: LOVE.

Because of its obvious power in the prevention and healing of life's emotional setbacks and trauma, I wonder how such a "thorough educational process" could overlook this most important natural component of psychophysiological well-being. It's no wonder why so many of us do not fathom this vital source of health and extension of fulfillment. We talk, write books and sing countless songs about love, yet it continues to be, perhaps, the most universally misunderstood topic; we rarely penetrate its exterior. What is love? How do you know you have it? How does one create and nourish it? These questions continue to go unanswered, much as we try.

Yet that doesn't stop any of us from investing time with and making commitments to long-term love relationships ... and we should. However, it wouldn't hurt to be more knowledgeable about this topic. Consider the idea that many of these relationships are bound by a fragile string; divorce is at an all-time high as one out of every two marriages dissolves. The gap between a couple's expectations about what they *thought* love was and what they *experience* is substantial. As a therapist, I see clients who are in pain over the issues of self-love and love of others. I am beginning to believe that love is the answer for practically anything; my graduate school professors would give me grief for such a global, "unscientific" comment. However, I'm willing to follow this strong intuitive feeling: When applied, love works! Reiterating the words of Beatles Lennon and McCartny, "Nothing you can do that can't be done ... It's easy ... all you need is love, love ... love is all you need." Learning to love our families, neighbors and friends, according to missionary Mother Theresa, is the way to stop the threat of nuclear war.

I do not pretend to be a world expert on the subject of love, but I have learned a great deal from the writings and seminars of people like Leo Buscaglia, Gerald Jampolsky and Ram Dass, and recommend their writings to you as well. Rather than delve into an academic query of why love works, I prefer to expose the practical side—how to act accordingly. I simply wish to reflect upon this subject to create an awareness of how it works, what it could be and how to make it a *modus operandi* for a joyful, gratifying life.

How this is accomplished is very simple, but it's not easy. You need first to align yourself with the law of nature that will create a life of love; in a word: GIVE. It is the law of reciprocity: If you want love, give it. To be in harmony with the Tao is to be compassionate and generous. Your power, according to Lao Tzu, is the result of passing love on to others. The Taoists call it Tz'u, which means caring or compassion in Chinese. In his translation of the *Tao Te Ching*, R. L. Wing writes about the power of compassion: "Leaders whose positions will endure are those who are the most compassionate ... They are able to make decisions with vision." Love and compassion reach all of reality and represent enormous energy to sustain life, a thought consistent with the teachings of the Tao.

These concepts harmonize well with the basic law of reaction in the physical sciences, as well: "Every action produces an equal, but opposite, reaction." Give love and it comes back to you. You can give away anything else—money, cars or other possessions—and they're gone; with love, it multiplies a hundredfold. The world mirrors your love. In describing the "evolved person," R. L. Wing's *Tao of Power* states it well: "The more they do for others, the more they gain; the more they give to others, the more they possess."

One of my first lessons with the law of reciprocity of love came to me at the age of forty. I'm a slow learner! My family is not very close; I hadn't seen my father for eight years—a long time to not share love with a person who played such a significant role in my childhood years. A basic lack of acceptance on both our parts was the contributing factor for our emotional distance. His living in Florida, far away from me in California, didn't help to narrow the chasm. While vacationing in Hawaii, he decided it was time to connect and called me. Uncomfortable with the relationship, I wondered how to "act" when he arrived. I talked with a woman his age and, with the wisdom of her seventy-three years, she told me to "simply GIVE; meet his needs—focus totally on him, putting your needs aside. Blend with his lifestyle." I couldn't have received better advice from the wisest Taoist master. I concentrated totally on giving love and anything else he seemed to want. Remarkable—for the first time that I could remember, my dad embraced me and said, "I love you." There it was—a clear lesson on love and harmony. I now feel so fortunate to have the chance to use this lesson with my two young boys.

The concept of GIVING is wonderfully exhibited on the mat in an aikido dojo. Two people come together and blend—one gives of himself with an attack of intent; the other receives and gives love through peaceful, harmonious conflict resolution. Blending with my dad became my aikido practice as he offered to me the opportunity for resolving our differences through non-force methods. Once again, the Tao was at work . . . *wu wei* in action.

Two years following that visit, my father died. I had seen him one week prior to his passing and I continued to relate to him with my heart. Through the practice of aikido, I am beginning to see how, with little or no force, I created the environment that enabled us to blend and resolve our long-standing issues as we both floated to "the other side." GIVING in this way has allowed me to trust myself and my world. Healing and love are possible if one only GIVES.

POWER OF LOVE

When I talk with people who have the advantage of wisdom from having "lived," I always ask the question: "Looking back on your life, what would you say is the most important aspect responsible for your happiness, joy and fulfillment?" Repeatedly the response is: the love they have received from family, friends and work. Yet so many of us are lonely, too afraid to open our hearts to others, at the risk of opening our entire world. Dr. Albert Schweitzer once said that "we are all so much together, but we are all dying of loneliness."

We all need each other, whether or not we care to admit it. Intimacy and love are crucial. As Barbara Streisand sang it, "People who need people are the luckiest people in the world," ... and the healthiest, too, I might add! People belonging to an accepting and caring community have a better sense of self-worth, lower levels of disease, less stress and even live longer, according to some studies. Bernie Siegel, M.D., specifically states that love has a tremendous healing power. In his marvelous book, *Love, Medicine and Miracles*, he writes of interesting work conducted at Harvard University by psychologists David McClelland and Carol Kirshuit. They show how movies of love increase the body's level of immunoglobin-A in the saliva, the first line of defense against colds and other viral diseases.

Other studies have found that socially isolated lifestyles contribute to illness and increase the rate of death threefold. Those with love and intimacy reverse this trend.

My personal feeling is that we may not live longer with love but, certainly, our lives will be more expansive. Love feels good and makes life worth living; the quality of your journey will be greatly enhanced. In addition, the following advantages make considering a lifestyle with heart worthwhile.

IMPROVED SENSE OF SELF. Giving love means receiving it from others. This recognition fuels the fire of self-image and confidence.

SENSE OF SECURITY. You begin to learn that security comes from within, and friendship and intimacy support a feeling of inner strength.

HEIGHTENED ENERGY. People who love feel positive and optimistic; these directly increase one's level of energy.

GREATER OVERALL HAPPINESS. The key to feeling joy is to give, and that's what love is all about.

IMPROVED CHANCES OF RISK-TAKING. You are more likely to risk change when people you love stand by your side and support your efforts.

LOVE DEFINED

If you were to consult a good dictionary, love would be defined as a tender, warm feeling of affection for, or attachment to, a person; good will toward others; a strong liking toward someone or something. Yet this is only one small part of the total picture. To act with love is to be tolerant, accepting, respectful, compassionate, optimistic, open, nonjudgmental and uncritical. It is an attitude of ABUNDANCE from which giving is possible. The flip-side of love is fear, where SCARCITY becomes the focus and generosity is unimaginable or unavailable. Fear creates a misalignment with nature's way as you become judgmental, suspicious, critical, defensive, pessimistic and unaccepting. Gerald Jampolsky, M.D. who wrote the book, *Love is Letting go of Fear*, articulates these thoughts well, and I highly recommend that you read it.

The important point is to understand that love goes beyond the mere expression of affection. It is an attitude or way of relating to your entire world, one that creates harmony and overall fulfillment at work, home or play.

TO ACT ACCORDINGLY

Remember that the law of nature states that if you want love, you need to give it. It's simple, but not easy, for many of us. I don't claim to be the sage of sentiment; I, too, must keep a constant vigil in order to align with this law in my life. It is work and perhaps that's why I've written this book. The following tools and strategies will facilitate the process of incorporating more love into your life. They will definitely increase the fun factor and deepen your level of daily satisfaction.

Relationships. The primary vehicle for giving and, therefore, receiving love is the relationship. This can be with yourself, another person or even with the work that you so proudly do. The key to success with relationships is to give without expectation. It is an attitude of unconditionality that blends with the true spirit of the law of reciprocity. For example, it's: "Daniel, I love you," not, "I love you if ..." Expectations are judgments and, therefore, not loving. They are a setup for disappointment and unhappiness. It is better to have preferences. Like the Samurai, expect nothing and be ready for anything. Couple this with flexibility and you create a powerful, positive situation.

I have noticed that the development of one good, solid bond with another will contribute to the growth of other relationships. It seems to teach you "the way," and this spreads to a variety of other situations. Don't try to reach all people in this world; this would be unrealistic. You can't force relationships; love cannot be legislated. Keep it simple and start with only a few.

Also, let go of the tendency to control a relationship; it's an impossible task. You can imprison someone's body but not his or her mind. Resentment will surface with every attempt to exert power over another. Paradoxically, the more you try to be possessive, the less you possess. The *Tao Te Ching* teaches us that the less we interfere with another's process, the more it will benefit us. Control reduces freedom and creates resistance. Ultimately, coercive tactics will destroy the relationship. We see this so clearly between parent and child. Parents live with the illusion that they can control their offspring; it only appears that way. You can set guidelines and boundaries, and with lots of love, hopefully, the child will dance with you to produce a life of harmony. This is the natural way.

Network. As a concept that has recently gained popularity, networking is a powerful method of giving love. It is a way to create a social support structure to share resources and talents. This helping process comes from the heart and attempts to make the world a better place in which to be.

One of the more powerful uses of networking is in the creation of relationships. Times have changed and so have the more traditional methods of meeting people. Meeting potential partners at clubs, parties, dances or bars is often unsatisfying and time-consuming. I favor, instead, an approach in which people network and match others who will likely be compatible. There are so many good people available, and this process increases the probability of bringing them together.

The goal of networking is simple: "Because I love you, I want you to have what you deserve, and I am going to give of my time to help you get it." This works well with any aspect of life and is most powerful when expectations are held to a minimum.

Listen. One of the most powerful gifts of love is one's time, in the form of listening. The message one clearly receives when listened to is "I count." It is a form of understanding, respect and acceptance; judgment, naturally, is withheld. In such a warm, non-critical environment, defensiveness is unlikely due to the absence of conflict.

The purpose of good listening is to resolve problems, achieve clarity, share joy and basically be available for others. In situations of conflict, it is a way to eliminate "losing" for all involved. It is the ultimate in communication.

Listening, like any other skill, can be learned, and many books are available on the topic. Universities and colleges teach courses on the subject that are worth the investment.

Aikido. The practice of many martial arts is the practice of love. This is particularly true of aikido where the protection of all involved is of primary concern. Rather than destroy life, it gives and nurtures it. Its focus is on the peaceful resolution of conflict. In the words of its founder, Morikei Ueshiba, "Aikido makes a fine flower of the soul bloom ... brings forth fruits and/or truth essence ... an art which is the ultimate good and ultimate love of this world. Aikido is love. The true martial art is to be one with the universe and to have no enemies. The essence ... is the spirit of loving protection of all beings."

As a student of aikido, I feel a warmth and acceptance from my training partners never experienced before in the more westernized forms of physical activities. As with the way of nature, love is created through balance, blending and harmony; the challenge is not a competitive one but rather to help each other learn ways to assert positive energy through love.

Forgive. This is, perhaps, the ultimate expression of love. It is an act of the heart rather than the head. To hold grudges or ill feelings toward another also creates inner strife and anxiety for you. Both parties suffer in this regard.

Forgiving does not mean you must love those in question, althouth love may be recaptured or ignited once the forgiveness process takes place and you experience inner peace. However, it's not a necessary component of the process.

Forgiveness is the releasing of the past and letting go of your fear of the future. It is an action that blends perfectly well with the Tao. Nature is forgiving; the child is forgiving, naturally.

Observe a child when he/she is upset with you. With no concept of the past or future, he or she quickly forgives and shares his or her love; no "holding on" occurs for these people. Children sustain happiness by releasing such tension and anxiety.

The key to forgiveness is to look beyond our egos and realize that, deep inside, we all have the same basic heart of the child. If we can see it in this way, forgiveness becomes a possibility. We all are humans and, by definition, make mistakes. We need to understand that our forgiveness of others' mistakes is really the forgiveness of our own when we behave in similar ways. I forgive you because, on some level, I am capable of doing the same thing. We are all, basically, children who need acceptance and love through forgiveness.

Risk. In order to create love and intimacy, one must be willing to risk vulnerability. Rejection is always a possible outcome of extending yourself to others, but the price for not taking those chances is a life of isolation without love. People often tell me that intimate relationships are frightening and potentially painful. They would rather protect themselves with a coat of emotional armor than risk getting hurt. What I notice, however, is that the real, true pain is actually from NOT getting close. In this way, individuals who won't risk create the very thing they try to avoid. Chapter Nine on courage can assist you in the taking of risks for the creation of love by putting the fear in perspective.

Children. Although they are probably unaware of it, children are wonderful models of love. Most kids give unconditionally, all of the time; and because of that, they receive endless streams of love in return. If we could follow this lesson, we would have similar experiences. Fear, however, makes it difficult to do.

I really didn't know what love was until I had a child of my own. We all have feelings of anger, frustration and discontent, but, unlike us, children let go, forgive and forget. Their love is pure and unadulterated. My most satisfying, joyous, happiest moments in life occur when I spend uninterrupted quality time with my children. It's difficult to realize that we were all that innocent and loving at one point in our lives, only to be subjected to the conditional realities of our world.

Another nice thing about children is how easy it is to hug and kiss them; with adults, there's too much ego and personality to transcend. Kids give us the opportunity to be spontaneous with our emotions rather than become absorbed in the analysis of all the possible repercussions of expressing our true feelings.

You should know that I was "dead set against" having children five years ago; I saw them only as opportunities to interfere with my life. Thanks to a determined woman, I was willing to risk the change, and I'm so thankful. I wonder how many other things in life I passed by because I saw them as hindrances.

Clearly, some of us would be better off without children and should follow our strong feelings. It's always a risk. If you think you'd enjoy it but feel hesitant, I'd encourage you to try. If I could have such a drastic turnaround in my attitude, you should have no trouble.

Visualize. Here is "old reliable" once again. To obtain love is to see your life in beautiful, loving ways through the soft eyes of your childlike self. If you "see" the world as a place filled with hate and malice, your images will directly influence your relationship to that world. You need to "see" the love and caring in order to feel it.

Imagine, in a deep state of relaxation, the kind of love you want in your life involving a spouse, friends, children, co-workers, career; "see" and "hear" yourself interacting with the qualities you feel are important to a loving environment. For example, perhaps you have been on a trip, and upon returning home you wish to experience joy and love. You could leave the outcome to chance, subjected to all the stresses of being away, or you could visualize how it would be with all the extraneous "garbage" put aside. Such imagery will help to put into motion all the psychological elements to insure that you'll experience a warm, nurturing environment. Ten minutes of positive programming on your way home could be all that it takes.

I use visualization often when I'm involved with people to maximize the chances of my focusing on love rather than fear; I try to see the heart, not the head. This works well with potentially volatile situations. It relieves the prior tension and anxiety I may have as a result of the possible impending conflict. Visualization can alter this negative scenario to one that will be positive and loving. See Chapter Three on vision for more detail.

Self-Examine. What qualities do you want from a partner in a love relationship? Make a list and examine whether you have these qualities as well. If you don't, try to develop some of them, because we tend to attract people who are similar to us.

In addition to this, be aware that you may keep love away because you feel unlovable and unworthy. Your self-critical nature precludes intimacy because you feel you "don't deserve it." These feelings of insecurity are transmitted to others in very subtle ways. You may really need to get some help to create an awareness of how you sabotage your efforts for love.

Communicate. Love is like a plant; it needs to be watered and nourished after being placed in fertile soil or it will die. The most effective way to nurture love is by open communication of feelings, verbal or nonverbal.

Nonverbally, a hug, kiss or even a slight touch will communicate the reassurance that love is alive and well. Bodily contact, if made appropriately, is the most powerful form of transmitting the feelings of love.

None of this is new; we need the reminder, however, because such behaviors are easily forgotten. Once a day, for a whole week, communicate love in these ways to someone close. If you do, you will realize three important things:

> how infrequently you use these methods
> how good it feels when you do
> how easy it is to do

REMARKS

So many of us are afraid to die. What I notice is that the idea of death is much more acceptable among those who have an abundance of love in their lives. The pain for those who struggle with death may be related to the remorse felt for not having loved more; the pain of not getting close runs deep. Ironically, such a lament prevents them from focusing on love in the present moment. Pain and depression prior to death could disappear if people could tune into others with their heart. Love is that powerful.

In his exploration of the power of love, Gerald Jampolsky, M.D., in his book *Teach Only Love*, describes a worthwhile experience on how giving is receiving:

> Sarah had been in pain with cancer for about four months. "Would you be willing to have peace of mind, if only for one second?" he asked. She said, "Yes, I haven't had peace of mind for years." Jampolsky replied: "Look at each person in this room and love them with all the love within you, expecting nothing in return." She agreed and he asked everyone else if they would focus full attention on loving Sarah for just one instant. When it was all over, at the end of the evening, Sarah stood up and said, "I can't restrain myself ... I have to tell everyone my pain is gone."

In that moment, she was not alone. She was completely involved in sharing love. How clear her example is—that there is no pain in love.

If you can extend your love for just one minute, perhaps you can gradually increase it until you experience it for a full day. It is possible. The law of reciprocity is a natural, universal concept. It applies to all circumstances, to all people, all of the time. If you give love, it will multiply a hundredfold and the world will be a more harmonious place. You simply need to begin with one other person and notice how it all comes back to you. "To give is to receive" is the way of life, the way you ultimately want things to be.

CHAPTER FOURTEEN

BEYOND LIMITED SIMPLICITY: THE ULTIMATE PARADOX

*Simplicity is the openness that
sees what will add to our freedom
or what will only complicate our
way.*

Hugh Prather
*Notes on How to Live in the World
and Still be Happy*

SIMPLICITY AND THE WAY OF NATURE

Looking back over the material in Part Two of this book, you can't help but be taken by its enormous simplicity. Nature is, by its very essence, simple; so it is with fulfillment. Yet so many of us fail to notice; we believe that in order to attain joy or happiness, we need to strive for multiplicity: More is better. Thus, we set ourselves up for one of nature's principal paradoxes, the law of simplicity:

Happiness, freedom and fulfillment result from limiting desires, not from having more. In other words, according to nature's way, less is more. Throughout the *Tao Te Ching*, Lao Tzu writes about the importance of returning to simplicity; the greatest happiness in life comes during the times of unadulterated simplicity. The chinese word *p'u* appears throughout the *Tao* and means "simple," "natural" or "plain."

In his book, *The Tao of Power*, R. L. Wing mentions that "simplicity in conduct, beliefs, and environment brings an individual very close to the truth of reality." He refers to simplicity as personal freedom: "It is really the absence of things that brings freedom and meaning into life." Simplicity adds to our freedom and that which complicates our lives detracts from it. Simplicity is the uncomplicated way.

You see it all the time. People become busy professionals, make more money, buy more clothes, purchase bigger houses and fancier cars, begin a family and complicate their lives. The more they "collect," the less free they seem to be. Friends of mine with a huge mortgage need to work long hours to make ends meet. Do they own a house or does the house own them? How free are they?

This isn't to say that possessions always complicate life. It is an individually determined phenomenon: One person's home is another's prison. As Hugh Prather intimated in the opening quote, will this "desire" add to your freedom or take it away? An assessment of each situation is mandatory. The purchase and use of a personal computer could save enough time to allow "freedom" to play; or it could become a workaholic's addiction, holding its "owner" in captivity.

So it isn't enough to despise all possessions and desires for the sake of simplicity. Acquiring what would make you comfortable and happy and give you more freedom in life is a wise choice. The key is to be honest with yourself and create a delicate balance between multiplicity and simplicity. Either extreme is, in itself, an excess that leads to an imbalance; and, according to the law of physical nature, any excess causes a decline. For example, whether you never have enough or you despise having any, money becomes an issue that interferes with freedom.

Misalignment with the law of simplicity means to be "hooked into" either of the two extremes. Rather than flow back and forth between the polarities, you rigidly adhere to either one, defending your position with righteous piety. In the process, you cannot blend or flow with new opportunities, and you become fixated with a limited reality. Your unwillingness to "let go" contradicts the Tao and all the laws of nature.

The concept of simplicity is foreign to many of us in the Western world. We were born and raised in environments where the concept of scarcity ruled, while achievement and accumulation were the tickets to freedom; or so we thought. Therefore, it's difficult to imagine how the "less is more" philosophy can create joy and happiness. Many of us still suffer from the "Depression mentality" and need protection for a rainy day.

Times have changed and we need to consider a major shift in attitude. Possessions are wonderful but do not assure us of joy or freedom. The advantages of a simple life are, themselves, simple . . . yet powerful. I am talking about the extraordinary spiritual freedom and peace one experiences from such simplification. I think about the enormous anxiety, tension and stress one absorbs worrying about their $50,000 car getting scratched. If you have nothing, you have nothing to lose.

I remember living in "poverty" during my student years—a hand-to-mouth existence. They were difficult times yet, in many ways, more joyous with less to worry about. They gave me time to contemplate my direction and determine priorities with sharp clarity. They were carefree, happy times—less emotional baggage, less chaos, less clutter. Relationships seemed to flourish as I had more time for them; my heart had more space in which to flounder. Although financial security was unattainable, I prided myself on an internal strength, a security that gave me the confidence to know I could make it with or without money. I felt no obligation to anyone but myself; no one owned me. This was a time of tremendous personal power and independence, a simple time, a free time.

However, the point needs to be made that, today, I would not consider this to be freedom. I can remember leaving graduate school and moving to Arizona with everything I owned in the rear of a Volvo station wagon. What an inebriating experience! The world was mine. I have exponentially more "stuff" and responsibility now, yet I feel much freer. With the support from my family, and a sense of roots provided by my home and friends, it becomes possible to be more creative, more diverse, more energetic. My present environment gives me the freedom to be me. Although my life gets "crazy" and out of hand at times, it is becoming more simplified. Because of that I feel I've reached a progressive state of happiness, a daily process of simplification.

By the way, I still have the same simple, basic, no-frills car I owned in school fifteen years ago. I'm not worried about scratches—or car payments either.

TO ACT ACCORDINGLY

Creating simplicity in a complex world, ironically, is simple, but not easy. It requires rethinking priorities and reevaluating lifestyles. Such change, if not done over a period of time, could create havoc and emotional upheaval. Shedding habits of complexity means determining how little it would take to get along, without sacrificing freedom and happiness. The answers to the following questions should help you to make sound decisions for the "shedding" process.

Do I really need it, this, them?
How will it help me be free?
How little can I get along with?

If it seems right, then possession will reflect simplicity; if not, then detach and "let go." And the adage "When in doubt, throw it out," becomes a viable option. In the words of songwriter Kris Kristofferson, "Freedom's just another word for nothing left to lose."

Changing from a life of complexity to one of simplicity is a risk worth considering. I would suggest beginning "simply" by shedding some of the unnecessary externals. The following should be a helpful guide.

Physical Simplicity. Do you need all those clothes? Perhaps you could give some away to people who really need them. How about expensive hair care? How could that be simplified? In the process of shedding these externals, you begin to touch upon inner issues, such as shedding vanity. This latter point was brought to my attention by Anne Lindbergh in her wonderfully sensitive book, *Gift from the Sea*.

Environmental Simplicity. Take a serious look at your home and ask the same three questions. We tend to crowd our living space with stimulating oddities that serve no function. Such "busy" environments can be distracting and interfere with a peaceful, soothing setting. I shed curtains, rugs, pictures, lights and furniture when appropriate. There is also less to clean as a result! For me, the less gadgets the better; something invariably malfunctions and it's annoying to fix it. The kitchen is a great place to start shedding.

Nutritional Simplicity. Take a close look at the average American diet and notice how terribly excessive and imbalanced it has become. There was a time when food was simple and the body got what it needed. We have become a nation of unsophisticated, ignorant eaters. Our "civilized" country has proceeded to destroy and mutilate its food supply through the use of complex industrialized methods. Witness the processed, refined, artificial products found on the shelves of any supermarket. Read the labels—see the additives; it's difficult to know what it all means. Most of the contents of these food products complicate your life in many ways, creating emotional and mental energy imbalances. What you eat (or don't eat) has powerful implications for many of today's problems: stress, depression, anxiety, cancer, heart disease, diabetes, allergies, fatigue, irritability, memory, clarity of thought, mental problems, muscle and bone injury, and hair, scalp and skin concerns, to name a few. Yet we overlook the importance of nutrition in creating wellness, happiness and fulfillment. The culprit is the perpetuation of ignorance and unconsciousness—even among those who are responsible for knowing.

I don't pretend to be an expert on these matters; however, I must say that an attitude of "back to basics" must be given a high priority. A simple diet of nutritious, real, whole food is the key. Grains, vegetables, fruits, nuts, legumes and other untampered-with products are a good start. Be cautious with alcohol, caffeine, sugar and salt consumption. Keep it balanced and simple. Moderation is a must; excessiveness, according to nature, is decline. (Read more about nutrition in Chapter Twelve.)

Relationship Simplicity. There are many ways to simplify your relationships. First of all, to enjoy friends, you do not need to spend enormous sums of money on dinner or entertainment. The idea is to spend time together, not to feel the pressure to cook lavish meals or eat at fancy restaurants. Some of my best moments with friends happen when we "pot luck" our dinner or go to an inexpensive restaurant with decent food. Once in a while it's fun to splurge, but on a regular basis, it gets terribly complex. Simple, home-cooked meals, followed by a home movie or table games, makes for a wonderful evening. Also, there's so much to do in the community that involves little or no planning; outdoor music, university theatre, picnics and nature hikes are simple yet meaningful ways to spend time with those you love.

Career Simplicity. Take a close look at what you do and ask the three questions. We often take on too much in our quest for money that is not needed, or for more recognition than is necessary. Evaluate your priorities. If family and leisure time are important, why do you continue to complicate life by including more career variables? Work is a primary source of stress in life and needs to be controlled if simplicity is to be achieved. Domestic work must also be included in this category; you need the balance at home as well.

Responsibility Simplicity. When you are a child, you think you want to have all of the responsibilities of adulthood. Then, as an adult, you realize that a balance would be the ideal. Many of us have too much responsibility because we feel that others couldn't do the job as well. This plays into the perfectionistic trap (see chapter on excellence) and causes life to become complex if not chaotic. Review what you do and consider delegating work and projects to others, at home or on the job. This will simplify your life dramatically.

Distraction Simplicity. We live in a world of distraction: the phone, the doorbell, noise pollution, chores, errands and much more. To create simplicity, avoid or alter these annoyances. For example, I turn the phone down and check for messages twice a day, rather than respond every time it rings. I create a work environment where I can control noise. I do my shopping chores during "off" times when the stores are less crowded; and I do more on each trip so I don't need to go as often. When I am home alone, I completely avoid the front doorbell; I know it can't be my friends because they come to the rear of the house. These changes simplify my life in so many ways.

Material Simplicity. According to the Taoist view, those who are materially oriented identify themselves only with possessions and have no other real purpose in the world. They are in harmony with death, not growth. Materialism and spiritualism are unlikely partners on the inner journey.

When trying to decide what material simplicity is for you, ask the three questions. Concentrate more on needs than wants. Remember that "balance" is the goal. Too many possessions complicate your life and distract you on the path of spiritual change and growth. Notice! ... that's all.

Simplicity is just one element of happiness and fulfillment, yet it is, perhaps, the most powerful. There's not much to say about it without becoming too complex. Nature is not complex; its laws are obviously simple and follow a very natural, logical pattern. There is a purity about nature that is best expressed in a simpler lifestyle. Our attempt to complicate our world, control it, conquer it, detracts from the peace, joy, harmony and fulfillment that is ours just by simply blending with "the way."

When times get hard, during moments of grief, sorrow, stress, anxiety or other inner turmoil, become simple by subtracting rather than adding: do less, eat less, think less. Let nature evolve so that you may, too. Avoid the tendency to fill your life with "things" and situations; this is the ultimate escape and complicates matters in the long run.

Lao Tzu taught that desires create havoc with the mind. As you let go of these longings, independence and power, paradoxically, are yours; detachment is the path to freedom. In his book, *The Tao of Leadership*, John Heider talks about strategies for a simple life:

> Use what you have ... quit trying to solve problems by moving ... changing mates or careers. Leave your car in the garage ... Sell the complex computer ... use pencil and paper. Rather than read every new book that comes along, reread the classics ... eat food grown locally. Wear simple clothing. Keep a small home, uncluttered and clean. Keep an open calendar ... let family customs grow.

If something makes you more free, attach yourself to it. If you want to be free, *learn to live simply so that you may simply live.*

PART

TRANS

What would it be like to live ac-
Chapter Fifteen will present a com-
way, a model for all of us who would
the transformation process can be.
enable you to use the valuable tools
seven-day period of incredible joy.
begin to live a life according to the
immediately.

WHERE

THREE

FORMATION

cording to the way of nature?
posite of the unlimited, fulfilled
like to see how realistic and simple
Finally, Chapter Sixteen will
learned in Part Two to experience a
By following this plan, you will
way of nature, the way things are,

WE CAN GO

BEYOND LIMITED LIVING: THE ULTIMATE POSSIBILITY

*Some of us see things as they are
    and ask, 'why?'
I dream things that never were,
    and ask, 'Why not?'*

George Bernard Shaw

THE UNLIMITED WAY OF NATURE

In his final book, *Tao: The Watercourse Way*, Alan Watts pays tribute to the incredible adventures of Thor Heyerdahl's *Kon-Tiki*. I had read about this journey years ago, but thanks to Watts, I see the significance of that voyage with respect to "the way." As I recall, Heyerdahl and his crew drifted from Peru to the South Seas on a lightweight, simply constructed balsa-wood raft. He literally went with "the flow," the natural flow of the mighty ocean. He had a very basic trust in himself and in the natural currents of the Pacific. As nature would have it, the salt water interacted with the balsa wood, creating a swelling that would bind the logs of the raft more securely. The ocean provided an abundance of food for nourishment. He succeeded because of the confidence he had in what the Taoists call *wu wei*—"not forcing," blending and going with the grain.

The "unlimited way" is the way of nature. It is a process, a trust; it's a way to "go about life" with all of its ups and downs. Like *Kon-Tiki*, we are put in the water at birth and told to make it. Unfortunately, most of the messages we get, from those who care to help, are misaligned with the great plan, the way it is supposed to be. Unlimited living is a path that facilitates blending with this plan. Harmonizing with the laws of nature, following the Tao, enables us to live a life of joy and fulfillment as it's happening.

According to the Taoists, the way of nature is the ideal way to go. It becomes the path of least resistance; the efforts to fight the way simply cause inner turmoil. The challenge of unlimited living is to blend with your world as it is, with all of its contradictions, paradoxes, absurdities and frustrations. You cannot change the way things are, but if you open your heart to the world as it is, you will be able to "see" things differently and, in the process, set the stage for living beyond limits. Your limits come from trying to manipulate nature and this, obviously, is futile. When you align your life with the pulse and rhythms of the world, you begin to see its purpose in the creation of fulfillment. In actuality, this path alone is, by its very nature, fulfilling.

PERSONAL CHARACTERISTICS OF UNLIMITED PEOPLE

The following characteristics describe people who follow a way of unlimited living. How well are you aligned with these features? Perhaps these examples could serve as guidelines to keep you on the path of nature. There are many people in this world who exhibit these qualities; one could even be your neighbor. Such behavioral characteristics are available to all of us. Notice ... and act accordingly. Choose a few to work on now; introduce them gradually into your life, and use the chapters in Part Two for support and encouragement. They will help you to synthesize what it would be like to live beyond self-imposed limits and to live a more fulfilling life.

Unlimited people still have the ups and downs, the emotional swings and whatever else nature has to offer. Unlimited people see limits as still there, but they are part of the natural way, a challenge to accept, examine beyond. The characteristic qualities of the unlimited person are:

> self-motivation and discipline
> sense of humor
> a sense of purpose, a reason for being
> pioneer mentality; will try new things
> vision; will see possibilities before they're real
> self-direction; inner focus
> deep concern for others
> self-love; his/her own best friend
> "limits" are to be questioned and transcended
> passion and love in what he/she does
> personal growth-oriented, as well as professional and
>   social
> takes risks; not afraid of the rough roads
> on the lookout for exciting opportunities
> learns from error, setback, failure
> knows how to prioritize
> pursues excellence; therefore does not procrastinate
> creates a balance between work and play
> knows when to "fill up emotional tanks"
> works with the ups and downs; knows the flow of life
>   is always in flux

uses networking as support for the journey of
fulfillment and self-empowerment

These qualities are in line with the Tao; balance, blending
and harmony are the cornerstones of these behaviors. Incorporate some of these into your world and create unlimited
possibilities. Complete integration will produce a life of extraordinary substance and fulfillment.

The time to start is NOW. If you had only one year to
live, wouldn't you want it to be filled with quality, happiness
and joy? The greatest fear is regret—regret over what might
have been. We all have individual journeys yet they can all
be fulfilling. These are "the good old days," the times you'll
think about in years to come. Talking with happy people, I
notice they have little remorse; they have taken the risks for a
full life and accepted the unchangeable outcome. Perhaps we
all could learn from this next statement of regret, spoken by
an eighty-five-year-old woman, Nadine Stair.

*If I had my life to live over again, I'd dare to make
more mistakes next time. I'd relax. I would limber up.
I would be sillier than I have been this trip. I would
take fewer things seriously. I would take more trips. I
would climb more mountains, swim more rivers.*

*I would eat more ice cream, and less beans. I
would perhaps have more actual troubles, but I'd
have fewer imaginary ones.*

*You see, I'm one of those people who live
seriously and sanely hour after hour, day after day.
Oh, I've had my moments and if I had to do it over
again, I'd have more of them. In fact, I'd try to have
nothing else. Just moments, one after another, instead
of living so many years ahead of each day. I've been
one of those persons who never goes anywhere
without a thermometer, a hot water bottle, a raincoat
and a parachute. If I had to do it again, I would
travel lighter than I have.*

*If I had to live my life over, I would start
barefoot earlier in the spring and stay that way later
in the fall. I would go to more dances. I would ride
more merry-go-rounds. I would pick more daisies.*

Essentially, Nadine is asking to return, once again, to those childlike, unlimited times. This passage was brought to my attention by a female student in one of my "Living Beyond Limits" classes. Her name was Marti and, thanks to her, I developed the exercise: IF I HAD MY LIFE TO LIVE OVER AGAIN. The exercise is, like the Tao, very simple yet amazingly powerful. To begin, project yourself into the future twenty, thirty or forty years from now. Imagine, as you enter the autumn of your life, how you feel about what transpired over the years. Ask yourself: "What would I have done differently? What do I wish I would have done?" Apply these questions to your professional, social, personal, spiritual and emotional lives. Dream about things that never were but could have been. When you arrive at some answers, ask yourself why you are not doing those things now. What could be done to put yourself in position to begin creating this life? In this way, you will be given the opportunity to "live life over" by doing what you'd like—now.

I wouldn't want to look back on life and realize that I had worried more than I needed to. Worry interferes with joy and detracts from a potentially positive outcome. Nature has its way and I can't fight it; there is a reason for everything. I do what I can to make sense out of situations and, beyond that, there's nothing I can do. This Taoist philosophy has silenced much of my worry and subsequent stress.

I recently realized that I would regret not having traveled to more interesting places. I generally enjoy being at home since I travel often for professional purposes. However, I need to consider various sojourns to exotic lands in order to quench the thirst for adventure.

And, as I mature, I become aware of my need to not waste time with "social games." I find that honesty and directness cut through the facade so often erected for "protection" purposes. I needed these games to survive in my youth, but I believe I can live without them now. The quality feels too good to wait for it. I am more inclined to be "up front" about my feelings and to be truthful about my needs. What good does it do either of us if I love you and fail to tell you?

There is a one-word solution to regret: BEGIN! Take the risk for unlimited possibilities by starting now. Follow the simple voice within, that intuitive self that speaks to you as naturally as a child; it knows "the way."

The way of life for most of us contradicts the Tao; we are on a path of constant resistance. We fight and force what we judge to be best, based on a set of antiquated, unexamined beliefs. Nature has the greatest influence over our thoughts and actions, and the sooner we begin to align ourselves with its rhythms, the sooner we'll experience natural fulfillment. The Tao reaches all of nature. In *Tao of Power*, Wing comments that "the Tao moves through the world, leveling the extremes, smoothing and harmonizing, and evolving the universe and all things in it." Passage thirty-four of the *Tao Te Ching* says it well.

> The Great TAO extends everywhere.
> It is on the left and the right.
> All things depend upon it for growth,
> And it does not deny them.
> It achieves its purpose,
> And it does not have a name.
> It clothes and cultivates all things,
> And it does not act as master.
> Always without desire, it can be named Small.
> All things merge with it, and it does not act as
>   master.
> It can be named Great.
> In the end it does not seek greatness,
> And in that way, the Great is achieved.

Wing's beautiful translation of the *Tao* allows us to grasp what's in store for those who align with it. In his words, such people "instinctively untangle the knots and smooth the fabric of life and allow the needs for growth, creativity and independence in those around them to be fulfilled." Lao Tzu, believed that to emulate "the way" would bring you into close harmony with the true meaning of life—a life of significance and fulfillment ... and limitlessness.

CHAPTER SIXTEEN

BEYOND LIMITED ACTION: THE ULTIMATE BEGINNING

Knowing how to create joy and harmony in life is wisdom. Implementing that knowledge is genius.

J. Cheng.
(Taoist philosopher)

 ### ACTION AND THE WAY OF NATURE

ecently I received a present that should simplify my life. It is one of those "hi-tech" multi-function phones that does everything but make breakfast. However, it sits on the table and gathers dust, failing to live up to its billing because I simply do not use it. Its life is limited—self-imposed—by me. The phone does not bring the joy it is capable of delivering.

So it is with most of life. As J. Cheng so wisely said in the opening chapter quote, knowing "how" may be wisdom, but using that awareness to act accordingly is genius. All the tools in the world will not build a house; and, all the tools in this book will not lead to fulfillment ... unless you take action. Simply begin!

The wonderful aspect to this journey is that it starts with the first step. Unlike so many of life's journeys during which you struggle over time to reach your goal, the inner journey is accomplished, with all its benefits, the moment you begin. Success is the process. When you begin to notice the Tao, the way and laws of nature, you can't help but live it because the outcome is immediate; it feels right.

Following the way of nature is a habit that becomes integrated into your life, impacting on all that you do. To develop this habit, you must train, like an athlete. The mind, like a muscle, needs to be "worked" in order to develop in this way. You need to train your consciousness and develop the discipline of thinking according to the laws of nature. I realize, as you probably do, that the training process may seem to be incongruent with the way of nature. It seems unnatural to "force" change in this way. To help with what appears to be a contradiction, think of the change process, "the training," as simply noticing ... without force. Once you notice, the switch will flow. You will want to create harmony with the way things are because it works; it feels too good not to follow. You will act accordingly if you just NOTICE.

I have a belief that says: If you could experience for five minutes the agony and pain of a severe, debilitating illness, you would alter those life habits that possibly caused the pain. Conversely, if you could enjoy the bliss of fulfillment for a similar length of time, you would, likewise, be more willing to alter your life to increase the chances of experiencing such joy. For example, unconditional love is its own reinforcer; you just need to encounter it and you'll increase the desire to meet with it again. This is one reason

why people have more than one child. They are more willing to invest their energies in that direction because of that
initial encounter with such incredible love.

Apply this belief to beginning your new journey. This
chapter was designed to facilitate your start. Notice I will not
ask that you change your life forever. That's too unrealistic
and, initially, overwhelming. I am convinced that if you
follow a program for just seven days, you will feel the power
of harmony, joy and fulfillment. From this beginning, you
will be in a position to decide where to go from there. My
prediction is positive: You will choose to follow "the way."

Before we approach the "SEVEN DAYS OF FULFILL-
MENT," I will ask you to take ten minutes, right now, and in
a deep state of relaxation, VISUALIZE what the following
means to you.

    HARMONY
    BALANCE
    BLEND
    NOTICE
    MODERATION
    PEACE
    LOVE
    SIMPLICITY

Notice how you feel. What does your body do? How did you
react? You can use this exercise each day, along with other
visualizations, to promote a life of wellness and joy. These
are the key words in the lexicon of unlimited beings. Practicing this exercise will enable you to recall wonderful images,
on the spot, by just repeating the word itself.

Now we are ready for action. Begin your "SEVEN
DAYS OF FULFILLMENT" only when you are ready to com-
mit to it; today would be preferable since this material is
fresh on your mind. If you wait a month or more, you may
lose motivation.

I will predict, with certainty, that when you follow

this plan you will have one of the most memorable, gratifying weeks in your life. I have asked hundreds of people to take the risk, and the feedback has been phenomenal. After a week's investment, participants felt enormous power and joy. A week is not very long. Remember to focus on the process; notice what you *do*, not what you get.

SEVEN DAYS OF FULFILLMENT

For the next seven days, practice each of the following at least once a day:

Visualize the day as you want it to be for a minimum of ten minutes. Consider suggestions from this book.

Risk one small risk, professionally, socially or personally.

Focus Spiritually for thirty minutes each day by reading a book of spiritual benefit, one that opens the heart. Prayer or meditation is also acceptable.

Affirm a number of powerful self-phrases and repeat them according to the guidelines.

Intuit and hear your inner voice for one hour each day. You might want to designate a lunch break or something similar as a way to remember.

Give whether through action or words, to those you love and give to them, consciously, at least once each day.

Believe by catching yourself using a self-limiting belief; write it on paper and change it to one that is *unlimiting*.

For your convenience, use the following check sheet as a way to remind yourself what's to be done and also as a progress reinforcer. Perhaps you'll want to create a larger one and post it in your room or on the door of the refrigerator.

I won't wish you luck because luck is a product of chance; following this program leaves nothing to chance. Have a wonderful week.

CHART

Parting Words

I have been influenced by many writers in the formulation of my thoughts. Perhaps the most noteworthy of these was the English bard, William Wordsworth, who had a very special relationship with children and a devotion to nature. It was his phrase, "the Child is the father of the Man," that has enabled me to begin seeing life through the unlimited eyes of the child; in parting, I ask you to do the same.

KEY

V-Visualize	I-Intuit
R-Risk	G-Give
S-Focus Spiritually	B-Believe
A-Affirm	

	V	R	S	A	I	G	B
MONDAY							
TUESDAY							
WEDNESDAY							
THURSDAY							
FRIDAY							
SATURDAY							
SUNDAY							

NOTES

NOTES

NOTES

NOTES

NOTES

NOTES